THE VOW

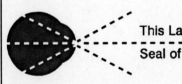

This Large Print Book carries the
Seal of Approval of N.A.V.H.

THE VOW

THE TRUE EVENTS THAT INSPIRED THE MOVIE

KIM & KRICKITT CARPENTER
with Dana Wilkerson

CHRISTIAN LARGE PRINT
A part of Gale, Cengage Learning

GALE
CENGAGE Learning·

Detroit • New York • San Francisco • New Haven, Conn • Waterville, Maine • London

GALE
CENGAGE Learning®

LIBRARY OF CONGRESS CATALOGING-IN-PUBLICATION DATA

Carpenter, Kim, 1965–
　　The vow : the true events that inspired the movie / by Kim & Krickitt
Carpenter with Dana Wilkerson. — Large print ed.
　　　p. cm. — (Christian Large Print originals)
　　Originally published: Nashville, TN : Broadman & Holman Publishers,
c2000.
　　ISBN 978-1-59415-420-1 (softcover : lg. print) — ISBN 1-59415-420-1
(softcover : lg. print) 1. Carpenter, Krickitt, 1969– —Health. 2. Coma—
Patients—New Mexico—Biography. 3. Husband and wife. 4. Carpenter,
Kim, 1965– 5. Christian biography—New Mexico. 6. Large type books.
I. Carpenter, Krickitt, 1969— II. Wilkerson, Dana. III. Title.
RB150.C6C37 2012
616.8'49—dc23　　　　　　　　　　　　　　　　　　　2012008965

Published in 2012 by arrangement with Broadman & Holman
Publishers.

Printed in the United States of America
2　3　4　5　6　　　16 15 14 13 12

ED172

DEDICATION

For keeping our circle of life revolving full of love and support, to our families we say thank you. Without our parents, siblings, in-laws, and children, our drive to continue on would have been greatly weakened. To our friends who have nurtured, supported, and loved us unconditionally we are forever grateful. To our children Danny and Lee-Ann, we are blessed to be the parents of such great kids. Remember to always do the right thing, give it everything you've got, and know that your parents will always love you and will be there for you. To our Lord Jesus Christ, you continue to shelter us, grant us grace, and bless us with peace, and you never ever turned away even when we sinned. Not a word can be spoken to the sacrifice you gave for us. For that we have eternal life and our love will never be forsaken.

CONTENTS

CONTENTS

PROLOGUE

December 1993

"Krickitt," her therapist began in a soothing voice, "do you know where you are?"

Krickitt thought for a moment before replying, "Phoenix."

"That's right, Krickitt. Do you know what year it is?"

"1965."

She was born in 1969, I thought, somewhat frantically. *That's just a little setback — nothing to really worry about,* I tried to convince myself.

"Who's the president, Krickitt?"

"Nixon."

Well, he was the president when she was born, I justified.

"Krickitt, what's your mother's name?" the therapist continued.

"Mary," she said with no hesitation . . . and no expression. *Now we're getting somewhere. Thank you, God!*

"Excellent, Krickitt. And what's your father's name?"

"Gus."

"That's right. Very good." He paused before continuing, "Krickitt, who's your husband?"

Krickitt looked at me with eyes void of expression. She looked back at the therapist without answering.

"Krickitt, who's your husband?"

Krickitt looked at me again and back at the therapist. I was sure everyone could hear my heart thudding as I waited for my wife's answer in silence and desperation.

"I'm not married."

No! God, please!

The therapist tried again, "No, Krickitt, you are married. Who's your husband?"

She wrinkled her brow. "Todd?" she questioned.

Her old boyfriend from California? Help her remember, God!

"Krickitt, please think. Who's your husband?"

"I told you. I'm not married."

1
BOY MEETS GIRL

"Good morning, and thanks for calling Jammin Sportswear. This is Krickitt."

When I called Jammin that fall morning in 1992, I had expected to be greeted by a bored-sounding customer service rep that would rather have been spending her morning doing anything other than answering a phone. But what I got was quite the opposite. When Krickitt said, "Good morning," it sounded like she meant it. And she even sounded like a cricket, all chirpy and upbeat.

"Hi, Krickitt," I answered her, "I'm Coach Kim Carpenter from New Mexico Highlands University. I'm calling about the baseball coaches' jackets in your catalog."

I have loved baseball from the time I was a little kid. I could always see myself coaching someday, just like my dad, so when I got my first coaching job with the Highlands Cowboys in Las Vegas, New Mexico, it was a dream come true. But even dreams have their mundane moments, and so I found myself ordering jackets for my assistant coaches and myself.

That first conversation with Krickitt was in no way the stuff movies are made of, but even so, as we discussed prices and colors, I got more and more interested in this telephone salesperson with the unique name. She was so refreshingly friendly and helpful that I couldn't help feeling like my day was better just from having spoken to her.

Our conversation ended, but I couldn't stop thinking about this girl named Krickitt. There was just something different and special about her voice and personality that I really couldn't explain. I could tell this wasn't just a job for her, it was more like a mission. It was as if she had decided to be the friendliest, most helpful person her customers talked to every day. If that was the case, then she was a roaring success in my mind.

I decided to call again a few days later to follow up on the order. "Good morning, and thanks for calling Jammin. This is Keri." Hmm . . . Keri. Not the voice I wanted to hear. I quickly had to face the fact that I was calling for a reason other than just checking up on those jackets. Keri sounded like a nice woman, but the fact was that I wanted to talk to Krickitt. I had to make it happen, so I thought fast.

"Hi Keri, I'm following up on an order with Krickitt."

"Just a minute." I could feel my heart racing as I waited.

"Hi, this is Krickitt. What can I do for you today?"

"Hi, Krickitt. This is Coach Carpenter from Highlands University. I called about a jacket the other day."

As Krickitt looked up my information, I had a few seconds to think. What was it about this Krickitt person that all of a sudden made me feel like I was a nervous, lovesick teenager? She was just a sales rep doing her job, and she was in California, *not* New Mexico, where I was. I pushed those thoughts aside as I asked her for some color samples before ending the conversation.

When the samples arrived, I spread them out on a table. My thoughts started going in unexpected directions. *Did she pick out these colors herself? Had she held the samples in her hands? Whoa, there! Settle down!* I couldn't figure out what was happening to me, or *why* it was happening. I was a grown man, after all!

13

I put those thoughts from my mind, yet I was unusually eager to talk to a certain telephone sales rep when I called again to order a purple and gray jacket. "Good morning, and thanks for calling Jammin. This is Krickitt." Success!

"Hi, Krickitt, it's Coach Carpenter. I . . ."

"Coach Carpenter!" She interrupted with a sense of excitement that surprised me, since she knew I was going to be ordering a grand total of one jacket from her. "It's great to hear from you again."

I wondered what she thought was "great" about it. Was it the prospect of another order, or was it because it was me? I tried to determine if I could sense more than a professional friendliness in the sound of that voice I couldn't get out of my head.

Unsurprisingly, I ordered the jacket. Then I ordered another one in a different style. When it arrived, it was so popular amongst the staff that every coach on the team wanted one, so I ordered some more.

A few months had passed since that first conversation with my favorite salesperson, and by now we spent a lot more time just talking to each other than actually conducting business. Then one day at the end of a call, Krickitt mentioned she wouldn't be working on the day I had been planning to call to check on an order, so she gave me her home number.

After that I started calling Krickitt at her apartment, and before long we stopped pretending the calls were about athletic clothing and spent the time getting to know each other. We often talked for more than an hour. No matter how long we talked, we never wanted to hang up the phone, even when my phone bill rocketed up from almost nothing to $500 a month. Those were the days before e-mail and texting, and few people even had cell phones. Krickitt and I were tied to land lines, but I didn't care about the inconvenience or the expense. She was more than worth it.

I finally found out the story behind Krickitt's unique name. Her given name was Krisxan (pronounced "Kris-Ann"), a name that reflected her Greek ancestry. The nickname Krickitt was coined when her great-aunt declared the two-year-old Krisxan could never sit still and hopped around all the time like a cricket.

It was no surprise to anyone that Krickitt was energetic and athletic. Her dad had once coached high school basketball and baseball. Her mother coached gymnastics, which Krickitt had taken a liking to from

15

the time she was old enough to make her way down a balance beam. In fact, she learned how to do a back handspring before she knew how to write her name.

I thought I was a sports fanatic, but Krickitt put me to shame. From kindergarten on, she practiced gymnastics every day after school in her mom's gym, and she put in five hours a day during the summers. At sixteen, she tore the rotator cuff in her right shoulder, but her orthopedic surgeon told her an operation would probably kill her chances for a college scholarship. So she suffered through and just kept at it, excelling in floor exercises and the balance beam. She didn't let a little pain stop her.

It was no surprise that Krickitt got multiple scholarship offers from schools with reputable gymnastics programs. She ended up choosing California State University at Fullerton, which had offered her a full gymnastics scholarship. She was a two-time Academic All-American there before giving up competition after she tore her Anterior Cruciate Ligament (ACL) during her senior year.

Though many of our initial conversations were about sports, Krickitt wasted no time getting to the spiritual part of our relationship. A few months into our friendship, she wrote this: "You said I can ask you anything, so I must be honest, Kimmer. You know that I am a Christian. Being a Christian is having an ongoing intimate relationship with Jesus Christ. I guess what I have been wondering this whole time is if you were a Christian too — if you had made the decision to ask Christ into your life to pay the penalty of your sin, and give you eternal life like he has promised if we ask."

Her faith was her life, and no matter what else she thought about me, she had to have a peace about my spiritual side before she could have any sort of relationship with me. As we talked through this part of our lives, we learned we were both Christians and had discovered Christ at the same age, but from that point our spiritual journeys had gone in different directions.

I was fourteen years old when I first learned about Jesus while at a friend's house. When I heard that Christ had died for me so my sins could be forgiven, it was the most awesome news I'd ever heard. I was so excited that I couldn't wait to get home to tell my parents about it. But when I started telling them what I felt, it didn't click with them at all.

My parents were nominal churchgoers,

but I don't think they had ever felt what I was feeling at that moment. We had never gone to mass regularly, although Grandma Helen took us when she had the chance. As a family we never talked about religion. But the message of Christ had touched me. It wasn't a quick process, but in time I came to fully trust and follow Jesus as my Savior.

Krickitt learned about Jesus from a little booklet called *The Four Spiritual Laws.* Its message filled her with excitement and curiosity, and she decided then and there that she would commit her life to following Christ. But no one else knew she made that life-altering decision on that day. She didn't even totally know, at the time, what that decision would mean for her life and for eternity. She didn't confirm her decision with anyone and didn't get involved in church programs at the time. When she started college, she finally got involved in a church, the Evangelical Free Church in Fullerton. While there her spiritual life transformed through the teachings of Pastor Charles Swindoll and College Pastor Steve McCracken.

During the summer of 1991, Steve led a mission trip to Hungary. Since Krickitt had just blown out her knee, she suddenly had time on her hands after years of daily workouts. When she heard about the Hungary trip, she saw it as a God-given opportunity to pour all the time and energy she had always put into gymnastics into something else. So she and her friend (and later roommate) Megan Almquist took on the challenge of being missionaries for nine weeks that summer. They had the incredible opportunity of spending time with and talking to people who were starved for Jesus' message of hope after generations of religious oppression.

I thought I was pretty faithful, but when I saw how Krickitt lived her life I was amazed. She had incorporated her faith into every part of her life. She wasn't a Christian just on Sunday mornings; being a Christian was the core of who she was. And I adored that about her.

My conversations with Krickitt kept getting longer and more involved. We also started writing letters back and forth. The letters were like the phone calls — we sent short cards at first but it wasn't long before Krickitt was writing me ten pages at a time. I can only imagine the length and number of e-mails we would have exchanged if we'd had that option in those days.

As is the case in any fledgling relation-

19

ship, it was inevitable that we would eventually talk about the idea of swapping pictures of ourselves, and early in the spring of 1993 we decided it was time to take that step. We couldn't send photos at the click of a mouse back then; instead we were looking at a long, nerve-wracking process of waiting for the mail to arrive each day. I mailed Krickitt a Highlands Cowboys media guide with my picture in it. Then I waited impatiently for a photo that would put a face to the amazing girl I had gotten to know so well over the past few months. I tried to convince myself I was just interested in her heart and her spirit; but at the same time, I figured it couldn't hurt if she also happened to be beautiful.

When the envelope from Krickitt arrived a few days later, I ripped it open and took my first look at a woman with dark hair, shining blue eyes, and a fantastic smile. I thought she was absolutely gorgeous.

However, it was obvious there had been another person in the picture, as I could see an arm around Krickitt's shoulder. Who had she cut out of the photo? Was it her boyfriend? Another "special friend" like me? My heart plummeted as I considered that option. *Take it easy, man,* I chided myself. *You're getting way ahead of yourself.*

I was dying to call Krickitt to see if she'd gotten my picture that day too, but I was a bit nervous about how she might respond. That night I called to ask. "Got it!" she answered. I didn't want to ask what she thought, so I just waited to see if she'd tell me. She did. "And you know, I thought, *This guy is even cute.*" We both laughed. I had been afraid the conversation would be tense and awkward, but thankfully it wasn't.

I mentioned that I had noticed she had cropped someone out of the picture she sent me. "Yeah," she responded. Again I waited, halfway dreading what I might hear. "I cut my girlfriends out because they're beautiful!"

We both knew what the next step would be: meeting in person. This would be a vitally important step in our relationship. After all, how do you know you truly connect with someone until you've physically spent time with him or her? So in February of 1993, Krickitt and I started talking about the prospect of meeting and spending some time together, short though a trip might be due to our work schedules. By that point we were talking more than five hours a week, and I figured a plane ticket wouldn't cost much more than what I was spending on phone bills. So I asked Krickitt if she'd like to come to Las Vegas and see my team play a few games. She said she didn't know. Before she decided, she would have to think and pray about it.

And she did think and pray. Years later, when Krickitt allowed me to read her journal from that time, I saw the evidence of it. One entry reads: "Lord, I really need your wisdom and Spirit to guide me with Kimmer. . . . Part of me wants to meet him — I think it would be fun. Part of me doesn't because I don't want to begin to have feelings for him if this is not of you. If it is, I pray you would show me that. I want to be led by you. I see so many ways in which we relate, but you must be the center."

Eventually, Krickitt leveled with me about her concerns in a lengthy letter. In a nutshell, she wanted to make sure we had no unrealistic expectations about the visit. She made it clear that at that point we were just friends. Her other concern was she didn't want to jeopardize my reputation in any way. As a coach and role model, I had a lot to lose if the situation looked to be something other than what it was — two friends meeting each other.

After two months of talking about it,

Krickitt made the decision to come to New Mexico so we could meet face-to-face. In preparation for her arrival, I reserved a room at a hotel for her near my apartment. I fully respected that Krickitt was saving herself for her husband one day. I realized that since I had fallen short, I would have to be upfront with her about my past, knowing that it would disappoint her. I knew also how important this was and I wanted to make sure that it was quite clear to anyone who might be watching that we were not spending the night together.

I made the two-hour trip to Albuquerque to pick her up at the airport. In those pre-9/11 days there were no restrictions on who could go through the security checkpoints at airports, so I was able to meet her at the gate. I spotted her the second she emerged from the jetway. I had seen her picture, so I knew who to look for, but I think I could have picked her out of the crowd even if I hadn't known what she looked like. I felt we had so much in common and had such a wonderful friendship already. Even though I already knew she was very attractive, when I finally saw her in the flesh I could hardly believe how beautiful she was. After all those hours on the phone, I finally had a real live person to match with that amazing voice.

Once we finally didn't have to worry about an astronomical phone bill, we talked almost nonstop all weekend. That first evening we talked about everything: our childhoods, our families, our jobs, our love of sports, our friends, and our incredible long-distance friendship. But more than anything else we talked about our faith. I already knew she was much more mature in her faith than I was, but I soon discovered that she didn't feel like she was superior to me. Instead she encouraged me to get to know God better and to follow him completely. She was so confident in who she was and in who God is.

After many hours we both stopped to catch our breath at the same time. In the silence, Krickitt glanced out the window. I saw astonishment on her face as she pointed at something outside. I turned to look and discovered that the sun had already risen. We had talked all night without realizing it.

The next day Krickitt attended the Cowboys' double-header, and both games were one-run losses. That evening, after the games, we talked again. I wasn't in an especially happy mood after the results of the day's games, and I got even more depressed while I told Krickitt about my mother, who was going through a serious illness. Yet for some reason I opened up to Krickitt in a way I never had with anyone else. I was amazed that she understood me and sympathized with me in a way I'd never felt before, and I knew then that this was something special. She wanted to know about my fears and challenges, and I wanted to discover the same about her.

I was surprised when Krickitt suddenly handed me a present. I opened the box, revealing a beautiful new Bible with my name embossed on it in gold lettering. I didn't know what to say. By the time I could mumble a thanks, Krickitt was already turning to the book of Job.

"Life isn't fair; it's life," she said softly, confidently. "Everybody has times when they feel like God's just not there. But he's always there, always bringing you closer to him, even when your mother's sick and your baseball team isn't playing well."

Krickitt started to read: "In the land of Uz there lived a man whose name was Job. This man was blameless and upright. . . ." After a while she stopped reading, and we talked about the terrible situations Job had to deal with. We asked the questions everyone asks about the man who lost everything. How could God allow such awful things to happen to such a good man? And perhaps more important from a human standpoint, why didn't Job throw in the towel and turn his back on God?

We took turns reading about Job, and we talked about many things as the hours passed and we delved into the incredible story of one man's faith in God in the midst of unimaginable tragedy. When we got to the end of the story, we rejoiced with Job as God richly rewarded his faith.

Sometime in the middle of the night we both fell asleep on the couch. The next day Krickitt flew back to California . . . and I had a hard time not falling asleep while coaching third base.

I later learned that when Krickitt's roommate Lisa dropped her off at the airport at the beginning of the weekend, she told Krickitt she felt like she was somehow saying good-bye to her for good. Then when Lisa picked her up at the end of the weekend, it was obvious to Lisa that it was only a matter of time before her roommate would be moving out.

There's no doubt we both had friends who whispered about our "spending the weekend" together, especially as Krickitt never slept in her hotel room. But we both knew that nothing happened that weekend that we wouldn't want to tell our mothers. Our time together had been so exhilarating, exciting, and amazing, yet all weekend I hadn't even kissed her. Believe it or not, I never even tried to. That wasn't what the weekend had been about.

When I checked my mailbox a couple of days after Krickitt left, I found a thank-you card. It was so beautiful it made me miss her more than I already did. I was struck by the way she wrote with such conviction and how my own feelings mirrored her own. This is what she wrote:

Kimmo,
I think back over this weekend and it was filled with so much laughter and tears — it was truly wonderful. I would never have imagined that we would be so compatible together. I enjoyed getting to know you this weekend. I feel so special to have seen who the real Kim Carpenter is. You have a heart that is so beautiful to me. Your lovingkindness, gentleness, humility, craziness, and uniqueness completely blew me away. The way you have opened up to me and trusted me with who you are and what you have been through means so much to me.

I, too, am blown away by some of the

things we have talked about. I prayed so much for our weekend together, that we would enjoy one another's company and have quality conversations. Well, I guess he answered that one, huh?! I have many questions and wonders with us. I am curious to know what is going to happen. I am ready to go with this relationship and see where it is going to go. It's not in our hands, Kimmer. I think we can go forward. . . . I'm scared, but risk is part of love. I feel that the Lord is either going to continue to open the doors for us, or he will shut them. I'm placing this in his hands and trusting him. Thank you for treating me so kindly and making me feel so special and adored.

Kim Carpenter, I adore and cherish you.

All my love,
Krickitt

Philippians 4:6–9 — Read and dwell on this.

The week after Krickitt returned home, we talked every day on the phone. We just couldn't get enough of each other. The next weekend I had some time off, and Krickitt quickly accepted my invitation for another visit. We spent the time talking, hiking, and four-wheeling up in the mountains.

I had a recruiting trip to San Diego a few weeks later, and I couldn't resist combining it with a visit to Krickitt in Anaheim. While I was there she introduced me to her parents, her brother and sister-in-law, and some of her friends. They were all so kind and welcoming — her father, Gus, and I hit it off right away. That wasn't surprising, as our baseball connection created an instant bond.

I went to church with Krickitt and discovered that her pastor, Charles Swindoll, was an incredible preacher whose passion for God was powerful and compelling. Going to church with Krickitt gave me yet another glimpse into who she really was as a person and as a Christian. The more I understood about her faith, the more I understood about her, and vice versa.

I returned to California in late May, but not without some apprehension. Krickitt and I had some serious questions to answer. Our feelings for each other were obviously deep and genuine but were we truly in love in a way that was leading toward marriage? I felt so much love for her, but I wanted to love her for all the right reasons and with all the right intentions.

We went out for dinner and then took a walk on the beach at Del Mar. It was nothing like our usual interactions, when we would talk about anything and everything for hours. This conversation was punctuated by long periods of silence; we knew the significance of this conversation and that every word was special and important.

There was no doubt we needed to make a decision about the future of our relationship. I couldn't imagine not having Krickitt in my life from that moment forward, and I hoped she felt the same way I did. But we had jobs and families hundreds of miles apart. It had only been eight weeks since we had met each other in person. Could we already be so sure we were ready to spend the rest of our lives together?

There were times that night when I thought we would have to end our relationship. It couldn't stay like it was. We could either go forward or we could end it. Should we go our separate ways now before we got in too deep emotionally, or was it already too late for that? Should one of us move? Should Krickitt quit her job? Should I quit mine? We had to decide, but it took us a while to work through everything as we walked hand-in-hand along the beach.

Eventually one of us brought up the idea of marriage, not in an excited or emotional way, but in a strangely calm way, as though it were one logical possible outcome of our relationship. We both agreed that it was where we wanted the relationship to head. But even though we decided that's what we wanted, it wasn't a done deal. Krickitt told me I would have to ask her father for her hand in marriage.

At the time Mr. and Mrs. Pappas were in Omaha, Nebraska, for the College Baseball World Series. I didn't want to have to wait until they returned home, so I called them at their hotel. Even though I had met Krickitt's parents and we got along well, I was, like any man in the same situation, very nervous about this most important conversation.

When Gus answered the phone, we exchanged some small talk and then talked about baseball for a few minutes. Finally, I took a deep breath and dove in to the real purpose for the call.

"Krickitt and I have been getting along really well. I want to ask her to marry me, but she said I had to talk to you first."

"She did, did she?"

"Yes, sir."

"Kim, we'd be honored to have you as

our son-in-law."

I was determined that the proposal would be creative. After I bought a diamond ring, I called Krickitt's roommates, Megan and Lisa, to help me set the stage for my visit. Their apartment had a security gate, and my plan was for one of the other girls to answer the buzzer so I could surprise Krickitt. They were happy to play along and easily got me inside the apartment complex without Krickitt finding out. I showed up outside their apartment in a suit and tie, despite my usual aversion to dress clothes. Then I started yelling Krickitt's name.

She soon came out onto her balcony, a modern-day Juliet in shorts and Nikes. I was holding flowers, a teddy bear with balloons tied to it, and a ring box. The unusual sight struck her speechless, but only for an instant.

"What are you doing here?" she yelled down to me.

"Well . . . Will ya?" I shouted back.

My heart dropped as she disappeared from the balcony, but it was only a second before I could see her flying down the stairs toward me.

"Will I what?" she asked expectantly.

I got down on one knee, looked her in the

eye, and asked the most important question of my life.

"Will you be my lifetime buddy? Krisxan, will you marry me?"

Krickitt took a quick breath and said the words I knew would come but was still dying to hear, "Yes, I will."

After embracing we stood back away from each other and after a pause asked, "Now what do we do?"

My original plan was that we'd get married the following spring. Krickitt admitted she didn't want to wait that long. I agreed with her thinking, so I tossed out a nearer date: Christmas. That was still too far off for her. So we set September 18, barely three months away, as the day we would become husband and wife.

I went back to Las Vegas to get the apartment ready for my future wife, and Krickitt jumped headfirst into wedding planning. She began making long-distance arrangements from Anaheim for a ceremony at Scottsdale Bible Church in suburban Phoenix, near her parent's home.

So on the evening of September 18, 1993, a perfect late-summer desert night, I stood at the altar with an audience of more than a hundred friends, family, and guests, held Krickitt's hand in mine, and made a vow:

"Krisxan, I've grown to love you very much. I thank you for loving me in the beautiful ways that you have, and I will always, always cherish this beautiful moment. I promise to love and respect you fully. I promise to provide for and protect you through times of challenge and need. I promise to be faithful, honest, and open; to devote myself to your every need and desire. Most of all, I promise to be the man you so fell in love with. And thank you, Jesus, for the blessing you have provided me in Krisxan. I love you."

Krickitt's self-created response filled my heart with thanksgiving and love:

"Kimmer, I love you. Finally today is here, the day that I give you my hand in marriage. I promise to be faithful to you, to love you in good times and bad, and to be equally ready to listen to you when you need to share. I promise to be open, and honest, and trustworthy, and I promise to support you each day. I'm honored to be your wife. I'm all yours, Kimmer. And I love you."

After we made our vows, the pastor asked my best man, Mike Kloeppel, for the ring. Mike reached under his coat, but instead of pulling out the ring, he pulled out a black, freshly polished baseball glove. Mike handed me the glove; I put it on and signaled to

Krickitt's dad, who gave me a big grin, stood up, and tossed a baseball up to me. I caught it, flipped the glove over my shoulder to Mike, and peeled back a square piece of white tape on the ball. There, inside the ball, was Krickitt's wedding band. Since a love of sports had brought us together, I figured it was only appropriate to mark our common interest in an unforgettable way.

The new Mrs. Kim Carpenter and I went to Maui for our honeymoon, and when we returned we settled down in Las Vegas, New Mexico, just as the new school year was getting under way. I started working with my baseball team, and Krickitt dove into her new life with the same enthusiasm, spirit, and faith that had made her such a great saleswoman. I had the luxury of still being in my same town at my same job, but my new wife had to start all over in a brand new environment. That was no problem for Krickitt. Before long she had become the team statistician, informal snack bar overseer for college games, and instant volunteer wherever she saw a need.

Krickitt also took a position as an exercise technician in Northeastern Regional Hospital's Center for Health and Fitness, a community fitness center on the campus of New Mexico Highlands University, where she designed exercise programs to help people reach their individual fitness goals. Her friendliness and gymnastics experience made her an instant hit with both the other staff members and the clients.

We decided that Thanksgiving would be a perfect time to make our first visit as husband and wife to visit Krickitt's parents in Phoenix. On Tuesday of Thanksgiving week, the night before we left, Krickitt and I had a quiet dinner and then sat snuggling on the couch in front of the TV. I had my arm around her, and she leaned her head on my chest. With no warning she looked up at me and asked, "Are you happy, Kimmer?"

I couldn't resist the urge to kiss her before answering, "I can't imagine how I could be any happier." And I kissed her again.

2
IN THE BLINK OF AN EYE

I looked up from the car and scanned the area for my wife of less than ten weeks. I was trying to figure out how to pack our car with enough luggage for our first Thanksgiving weekend with Krickitt's parents and still leave room for the two of us plus one of the members of my coaching staff who was hitching a ride to the airport in Phoenix.

"Hey, Krick, you gonna take all day?" I yelled toward the open door to our apartment.

"Here I am," Krickitt announced as she appeared in the doorway. She practically hopped down the sidewalk toward me, just like the insect her aunt had compared her to all those years ago. I couldn't help but watch her as she approached me.

"I love you, Kimmer," she said as she reached me, suddenly uncharacteristically still. "I love you, Krickitt," I answered. While Krickitt wedged a few more bags into the trunk, I went back for one last look to see if we'd left anything, then locked and closed the door behind me.

As I headed to the car, I thought for a few moments about the amazing things God had given me over the past few years, most notably a new job and a new wife. I couldn't believe that two months had passed since Krickitt and I had been on our honeymoon, enjoying the warm sand and tropical paradise of Hawaii. Now we were headed off for the Thanksgiving holiday, and Christmas was just around the corner. Time was moving too fast. I wanted to enjoy every day and I looked forward to starting many new traditions with my wife as we celebrated our first major holiday together.

"Hey, Kimmer, you gonna take all day?" Krickitt tried to be serious, but she couldn't do it for long and soon broke out into a huge smile. We laughed as I slipped into the driver's seat. I started the car, backed out of the parking lot, and eased into the holiday traffic.

We had a long trip ahead of us, but it was a relatively easy one from our home in New Mexico. We would have interstate highways the entire time as we made our way through Santa Fe, Albuquerque, and Flagstaff, finally ending in Phoenix. Originally we had planned to leave in the morning in order to get to the Pappas house before dark, but our passenger wasn't able to leave until after lunch. By the time we picked him up and headed southwest on I–25, it was already after two o'clock. It was going to be close to midnight by the time we pulled into my in-laws' driveway, but Krickitt and I didn't care. This was our first official holiday as husband and wife, and nothing mattered as long as we were together.

We sailed through Santa Fe and Albuquerque, but soon after we turned west on I–40 toward the Arizona border, I started feeling as if I was coming down with a cold. I tried to ignore it, because we had a long way to go, but Krickitt noticed something wasn't right. She asked if I was okay. I told her I wasn't feeling quite right but that I'd be fine in a few minutes.

But I wasn't fine in a few minutes, I was worse. By the time Krickitt said we ought to stop for some medicine, I was in no shape to argue with her, so we made a quick pit stop to pick up what I needed.

"Maybe I should drive for a while," Krickitt suggested. "I don't mind. Then you can lie down in the back seat and get some rest."

I felt truly awful, so I had no problem taking her up on her offer. "That would be great." I sighed before adding, "This sure isn't how I planned to impress the in-laws on our first holiday with them."

Krickitt flashed me her signature smile; I smiled back as well as I could, but it didn't compare. She took the wheel with our passenger by her side while I tried to stretch out in the back. Our Ford Escort was brand new but wasn't designed for a grown man to sleep in the back seat. However, with an eye more to comfort than safety, I realized I could fold down the back seat and stretch my legs out into the trunk. I did my best to get comfortable while I waited for the medicine to kick in.

Just past six in the evening we passed through Gallup, the last big town before the New Mexico/Arizona border. Darkness was falling fast, and Krickitt turned the headlights on. I finally got into a somewhat comfortable position and dozed off with my head at the back of the driver's seat and my legs toward the back of the hatchback. Suddenly I was jolted awake by a firm yell of, "Watch out!" as the car quickly decelerated and swerved to the left. I rose up just in time to feel the impact thrust me into the back of Krickitt's seat. Having slid my head off her seat toward the driver's door, I looked in the driver's side mirror and could see headlights zooming toward us, getting larger and larger and then completely filling the mirror in a split second.

My wife let out a bone-chilling scream.

The highway patrolman's report said that at approximately 6:30 p.m. on November 24, 1993, 5.7 miles east of the Arizona/New Mexico state line, a white Ford Escort was involved in a collision with two trucks. Later investigations revealed that a red flatbed truck with a load of car parts had started having engine trouble as it traveled west on I–40. As a result, the driver slowed to about twenty-five miles per hour in the right lane. Traveling at a normal interstate speed, Krickitt came up behind the truck, which was hidden in a cloud of black smoke produced by a defective fuel filter. During the day, the smoke would have been visible, but as night had fallen, Krickitt had been unable to see it from a distance.

Though the flatbed's emergency flashers weren't on, Krickitt eventually saw slow-moving taillights loom into view through the exhaust cloud, braked hard, and swerved to the left. At the same moment a pickup truck following too close behind our car closed in on us.

The right front fender of our Escort

clipped the left rear corner of the flatbed. Then as the car started to spin and Krickitt struggled for control, the pickup came from behind and rammed into the driver's side of our car. The impact sent our car careening into the air. It sailed thirty feet, slammed back to the ground, rolled one and a half times, then slid upside down for 106 feet and stopped on the shoulder of the road.

After we were hit, I don't remember hearing anything or feeling any immediate pain, but I recall every sensation of movement that took place from the moment of impact until our car came to a stop. My face was suddenly jammed between the driver's seat and the side of the car. My head was jerked back. Then I rolled over to the other side of the car, where my rib cage hit the wheel well. Next I experienced a momentary floating sensation, a slow-motion twisting and tumbling like the dream sequence in a movie. I saw sparks and thought the car was on fire. Finally, I felt a strange tingling sensation in my back. Then everything was still.

I was too stunned to say anything for a few seconds while my brain started to clear. When I could think again, I didn't think about the chance that I might be hurt. I couldn't feel a thing. All I could think of was my wife.

"Krickitt!" I screamed. I was answered with silence. "Krickiiiiitt!!" I knew I could hear, because I recognized the sound of the car engine running. But my wife of two months was not answering me. I took a few seconds to look around and get my bearings. After a second I realized the car was on its top and I was lying inside on the roof. The sunroof had been shattered during the long, final skid, and I had made the last part of that 106-foot trip on broken glass and pavement.

Once again I screamed for my wife, and as the sound of my voice died away, I felt something wet on my face. After the ride I'd just taken, I figured I was probably cut and bleeding. I tried to raise my hand up to my face to feel for injuries. I saw my hand slowly come toward my face, dreamlike, as if it were somebody else's hand. As it got closer a red splotch appeared on it, then another. The hand itself didn't seem to be hurt, so I figured the blood was somehow coming from a cut on my head.

I tried to stop the splotches by holding my hand away from my face, but they kept coming. The blood ran down my arm and started dripping down onto the broken sunroof. I finally looked up. It was a strange sensation to see everything upside down, seatbacks pointing down at me, no windows where they should have been.

My still-muddled mind finally deciphered that the dripping blood wasn't my own. Overhead, my wife was suspended upside down by her seat belt. Her arms dangled limp. Her eyes were closed. She didn't move. We weren't more than a couple of feet apart but I couldn't reach her. Since it was almost dark, I couldn't see her clearly enough to tell what sorts of injuries she might have. I suddenly realized that she might even be dead.

"Krickitt!" I snapped in my hard-nosed coach voice, hoping to shock her into waking up. Her eyes didn't open, but she stirred a little. Then she let out a long, ragged, sighing breath and was still again.

I thought I had just heard the last breath my wife would ever take.

I called her name again and started trying to get out of the car, but I couldn't move and at first I couldn't figure out why. There wasn't anything on top of me or in my way, and I had a clear shot out of the car through the rear window next to me since the glass was completely gone. After a few moments I realized I had no feeling in my legs. I was unable to move from the waist down.

My nose started to tingle, so I reached up to touch it. I felt something sharp. I was shocked to discover that it was the bone at the base of where my nose should have been. Lower on my face I felt what I first thought was a badly swollen lip. It was not. It was my nose, hanging down in front of my mouth by a flap of skin.

At last I heard another voice, but it wasn't Krickitt's. "Give me your hand! I'll help you out!" I turned to the window and looked straight into the face of a stranger, our very own Good Samaritan.

"I can't move my legs," I shouted back.

"Turn the motor off! This thing could explode any minute." After a moment of confusion, I realized the man was talking to our passenger, who had been riding shot-gun. Somehow he had made it through that whole ordeal with only a separated shoulder. Though he had been a bit dazed, he had been able to get out of the car, and at the stranger's command he reached back in to get to the ignition.

"The key's broken off," he said.

"You've got to get it turned off!" the stranger demanded. After some desperate jiggling and twisting, the ignition switch turned and the engine fell silent.

"Okay, I'm coming in to get you," the man said. Dropping to his stomach, he army crawled through the window beside me. I grabbed him around the shoulders, and he held on to me with one hand while he used the other to help scoot us backward out of the car and over to the grass beside the highway.

I saw then that another vehicle had stopped. A husband and wife headed toward us, leaving their children in their van. "You kids stay inside and pray," the man instructed as he approached our car. He looked around at all the wreckage and blood and, without any show of panic or defeat, put his hand on one of the upturned tires and started praying. His wife came over to me in the grass to see what she could do to help. She was afraid I was bleeding to death until she discovered much of the blood on me wasn't my own.

The couple introduced themselves as Wayne and Kelli Marshall and offered to do whatever they could to help. At the moment, the only thing I needed was to know that my wife wasn't dead.

As my rescuer wrapped me in blankets from his truck cab, another car stopped and the driver hurried over to me. She said a few words, then stopped abruptly with a look of horrified recognition on her face. "Oh my goodness! You're Danny Carpenter's son! Your cousin Debbie is my best friend! I'll get in touch with your family," the woman said and left the scene to start making calls.

I couldn't help but be amazed at how God was already taking care of us. There we were in the middle of nowhere and we had already encountered a rescuer, a prayer warrior, and a family friend.

The drivers of the other two vehicles involved in the crash had no visible injuries, and the two passengers in the pickup only had relatively minor wounds. The same could not be said of Krickitt and me. Not only was I in bad shape physically; I was also numb with shock. All I could think about was Krickitt trapped inside the twisted-up car a few feet away, looking like she was either bleeding to death or already dead. Her head was caught between the steering wheel and the roof where the top had been crushed during the rollover. I realized that if I'd been driving I would have been killed instantly, because I wouldn't have fit in the space remaining after the impact and my skull would have been crushed. But in Krickitt's case, we could see that unlatching her seat belt before her

47

head was free would probably break her neck if it wasn't already broken.

Within minutes the police and ambulances started arriving. It was obvious that Krickitt would have to be cut out of the car, but the EMTs were afraid to wait that long to start treatment. So one of them, DJ Coombs, crawled inside the car — not mentioning that she had severe claustrophobia — and started giving Krickitt IVs and monitoring her vital signs as she was still hanging upside down from the seat belt. Krickitt seemed to drift in and out of consciousness; her pupils alternately constricted and dilated — a classic symptom, I later learned, of severe brain injury.

While the rescue team was still cutting open the car, our passenger and I were loaded into an ambulance. On the way to the hospital in Gallup, the EMTs began cataloguing my injuries. My left ear was almost torn off; my nose was nearly severed. I also had other facial lacerations, a concussion, two cracked ribs, and a broken hand. Doctors would later discover a scraped lung and bruised heart muscle.

As we sped along, I heard the ambulance attendant call the hospital on the radio. "We have two male accident victims, one in critical condition, one serious. The third victim

48

is still at the scene in severely critical condition." That didn't sound good, but I realized that it at least meant Krickitt was still alive.

When we arrived at the emergency room of Rehoboth-McKinley Christian Hospital in Gallup, I was immediately taken to get an X-ray and CT scan. The medical personnel had discovered a big knot behind my left ear that they thought might indicate a skull fracture. When I was finished, Krickitt was already being given life-saving treatment in another area of the ER, so I didn't see her, but I knew the news wouldn't be good. After all, I had seen her in the crumpled car, and it had taken them more than half an hour to cut her out of it.

Nobody would give me a straight answer about Krickitt's condition. How was she doing? Was she going to recover? Was she going to be okay? Nobody would tell me, which I realized was not a good sign. I later learned that when one of the ambulance technicians heard Krickitt was still alive hours after being admitted to the hospital, she refused to believe it. She had never seen anyone survive such massive head trauma.

As soon as Krickitt had arrived at the hospital, the medical staff turned all their attention to her, which didn't draw any complaints from me. The ER team had given me some preliminary treatment, but I didn't want to take any sedative or have any other work done until I knew what was happening with my wife. I had been waiting for a while when a doctor approached me. His manner was professional and confident, but when I looked in his eyes I could tell he was exhausted. He handed me a little manila envelope.

"Mr. Carpenter, I'm terribly sorry."

I couldn't formulate a response before the doctor left the room. There was nothing to do but investigate the contents of the envelope. I opened it with my good hand and slid the items out into the broken one. I stared down at the Highlands University watch I'd had made for Krickitt . . . and her wedding ring.

When I gave her that ring, I had made a vow to protect her through times of challenge and need. This was definitely a time of both challenge and need, but I felt helpless. There was nothing I could do to protect her now.

My thoughts and feelings were all scrambled up inside me. I was in pain, and I was exhausted, but most of all I was annoyed that I didn't know how Krickitt was doing. But all of a sudden, piercing through everything else, was the thought that she was dead.

I was too incredulous to be sad. It wasn't that I wasn't willing to believe my wife was dead; I *couldn't* believe it. I was incapable of accepting the fact that those blue eyes were closed forever and I would never again see her smile shining at me from other side of the dinner table. I couldn't believe that the most joyful, most enthusiastic woman I had ever known could be torn from my life so savagely. My brain simply refused to process the idea that after two months of marriage I was a widower. A *widower.*

Some time later a nurse came in to check on me and update me on Krickitt's status. "We've done all we can, and she hasn't improved," she explained. "She's beyond medical help." *Maybe she's beyond medical help,* I thought, *but she's not beyond God's help.*

The nurse continued, "Still, she's hanging in there better than anybody thought she would. She's strong, and she's in excellent physical condition. The doctor has put in a call for an airlift to Albuquerque." The door that had seemed shut and sealed only minutes ago had miraculously opened a crack.

At the time I didn't know it, but when the medical flight team got orders to fly my wife

130 miles to the University of New Mexico Hospital in Albuquerque, they were afraid, based on their experience, that it would be a wasted trip. It would take a solid hour for the helicopter to get to Gallup, and then it would be another hour before they could get my wife back to Albuquerque. By then they figured it would likely be too late. Krickitt would be dead.

But by God's grace, the staff at Rehoboth-McKinley Christian Hospital in Gallup took a chance on Krickitt Carpenter. As they wheeled her out of the emergency room to get ready for the flight, I saw her for the first time since I had been taken away from the scene of the accident hours before. She was lying on a gurney, surrounded by medical staff that were keeping track of what looked like about a dozen IV lines and monitors. My wife's head and face were so swollen and bruised that I could barely recognize her. Her lips and ears were blue-black, and the swelling was so bad that her eyelids couldn't close all the way. Her eyes looked to the right with a blank stare, and her arms moved around aimlessly (more signs of severe head injury). Her body temperature was unstable, so they had put her in a big thermal wrap. To me it looked like a body bag.

I got up off my bed and grabbed both of Krickitt's hands. They were shockingly cold. "We're gonna get through this, Krick," I said to her. "We're gonna make it." I smiled but felt the tears coming just the same. "Don't you die on me!" I pleaded, my mouth inches from her face. She was wearing an oxygen mask and I could hear her breathing, shallow and tentative. "We're in this forever, remember? We've got a long way to go!"

When they began wheeling Krickitt's gurney out to the helipad, I suddenly realized they had no intention of taking me with them. "They have to have two medics and a lot of gear to give your wife any chance for survival," someone explained to me. "There's no room for a passenger."

I wasn't a passenger; I was her husband. I was also a patient, I suddenly realized, with fairly severe injuries of my own. I tried to convince anyone who would listen to get the helicopter to come back for me. But that wasn't to be. Someone told me there were two other active calls at the time, and there was no time to make another two-hour round trip for me. As this registered, I helplessly watched my wife get wheeled through a set of swinging doors toward the waiting helicopter.

"Hang in there, Krickitt! I'm praying for you!" I yelled, before I started sobbing as I watched the love of my life be rolled up to the waiting helicopter and eased inside. I stood there in disbelief as the rhythmic sound of the copter's overhead rotor faded into the distance.

From the moment I had arrived at the hospital, I had tried repeatedly to get in touch with Krickitt's parents in Phoenix and mine in Farmington, New Mexico. But since it was the day before Thanksgiving, nobody was home. Running out of options, I finally called Krickitt's old phone number and talked to her ex-roommate Lisa, who still lived with Megan in the apartment the three of them had once shared in California. I quickly explained the situation, then asked her to try and reach Krickitt's parents, tell them we'd been in a wreck, and stand by for further news.

Next I called my boss at the university, athletic director Rob Evers. I told him the situation and asked him to track down my parents. He said he'd take care of it and immediately started on the trail. He knew I had an uncle in Albuquerque with the last name of Morris, but he didn't know my uncle's first name because everyone called him by a nickname, Corky. So Rob called the telephone operator and explained that he had an emergency and had to contact the family. "We don't usually do this," the operator explained, "but stay on the line." She called every Morris in Albuquerque until she found the right one.

Uncle Corky had a phone number for my dad's business partner. Rob called the man, who was eventually able to get in touch with Dad on his cell phone. He and Mom were in Roswell, New Mexico, where they were spending Thanksgiving with my brother Kelly. Dad called immediately. I told him that a doctor had just given me Krickitt's wedding ring and a, "Mr. Carpenter, I'm terribly sorry." I was frustrated that I didn't know what was going on, but I would let him know when there was any news.

As I lay there after Krickitt's chopper took off, I still couldn't believe that my wife of two months was going to die. She was so full of life, so joyful, so focused on being the woman God wanted her to be. Just that morning she had been writing in her journal again. When I read the entry later, I was amazed by what she wrote that day: "Lord, . . . Help us to have endurance to work hard for your values. I pray for opportunities to serve you, be a witness for you, be a leader for you. . . . Please open my heart and Kimmer's to do the things that will be pleasing to you." Little did we know on that Thanksgiving Eve how God would answer those prayers in amazing and extremely difficult ways.

But that night my thoughts weren't on the future. They were focused on the horrific events of the present. I called my dad again. Through my heartbreaking sobs, I managed to gasp out the words, "They've flown Krickitt to Albuquerque and they wouldn't let me go with her. You've got to come and get me. Take me to her." I broke down again, overwhelmed by the emotions flowing through me. "I have to see my wife again before she dies."

3
A MODERN-DAY MIRACLE

While my dad was figuring out how to get me to Albuquerque, Krickitt's parents were just arriving home to an empty house. Gus and Mary had done all they could to make sure our first Thanksgiving as a married couple would be special. Since we weren't going to be able to make it to their house for Christmas due to my work schedule, they decided to add an early touch of holiday cheer to their house by putting up their Christmas lights, both inside and out. They knew we wouldn't be getting in until late in the evening, so they had gone out to watch a basketball game.

Krickitt's parents hadn't yet heard the news when they returned home from the game, but Mary knew something was wrong even before they entered the house. It was after midnight, yet when they pulled in the drive there was no white Escort sitting there to announce our arrival. They soon heard the life-altering news: their beloved daughter and her husband had been in an accident and the outlook wasn't good.

I was waiting for my dad to call back with his plan when Mary called me. Since Krickitt was on her way to Albuquerque, I couldn't tell Mary how she was doing, as I didn't know myself. But I do remember telling her, "I'm hurting bad and I can't live without her." Mary said she would call the hospital to check on Krickitt's status, and they would catch the first plane out of Phoenix in the early morning hours of Thanksgiving Day.

It could have been two minutes or two hours after talking to Mary that my phone rang again. I answered and heard my father's voice. "Son, how are you doing?"

"I want to see Krickitt, that's how I am. I can't breathe and my back is killing me. I have to see her, Dad." The tears were pricking in the back of my eyes, but I had to keep them under control to get through this conversation. I hoped with all my might that Dad could get me to Albuquerque to see my wife.

He could. "Listen, son," he said in a steady, controlled voice that gave me both strength and comfort, "I'll drop your mother off at the hospital in Albuquerque. Then I'll meet you at the truck stop in Grants and drive you back to see Krickitt."

Dad made it sound like he would only have to make a quick trip across town. But the truth was that he and Mom had just driven almost four hundred miles across New Mexico to get to my brother's house. Now he was going to drive two hundred miles from Roswell to Albuquerque and then another sixty to Grants, the midway point between Albuquerque and Gallup. To top it all off, a storm had blown in during the night, and some sections of the highway were solid sheets of ice.

"The problem is that I don't think I can get out of here unless you come and get me discharged. They admitted me through the ER, and they haven't done much for me yet because they were so busy with Krickitt. I'm in pretty bad shape, Dad."

"I'll send Porky to get you out."

When I heard that, I knew it was done. Porky Abeda was one of Dad's best friends, a big bear of a man and former fire chief of Gallup. He was well known in the town and a very persuasive man, so I knew if anybody could get me out of the hospital, Porky could.

Understandably, the medical staff members did not agree with my decision to leave.

A nurse tried to reason with me, "We haven't had a chance to examine you for internal injuries. It is not advisable to leave now."

"I just want to be with my wife."

"By the time you get to Albuquerque, it may be impossible to repair the damage to your nose and your ear. And we don't even know what kind of internal bleeding you might have." The nurse paused and gave me a very stern look. "If you leave the hospital now, you could die."

"I don't care," I replied. "If Krickitt dies, I don't want to live."

If a patient wants to be discharged against medical advice, the hospital is only supposed to release him or her to a relative. Porky doesn't look like he could be my cousin, uncle, or any other relation. He's full-blooded Navajo and I'm Caucasian. I don't know what he said to the hospital staff, but it worked.

After the papers were signed, Porky wrapped me in a blanket, packed me into the back seat of his car, and took off for Grants. I tried out various positions in the back seat, trying to find one that would allow me to breathe with less pain. Every time I inhaled it felt like my chest was on fire. Looking up through the window, I watched the lights as we zoomed down the interstate. I finally saw the huge truck stop sign at Grants, and we pulled off to meet my dad.

He was pacing on the sidewalk. He had made the drive from Roswell in about half the normal time even though the highway was coated with ice and there had been two other major wrecks between Albuquerque and Gallup that night — the same wrecks that tied up the helicopter that I had hoped would take me to Albuquerque and Krickitt. Porky hopped out of the car and I watched Dad walk up to him.

"Where's Kim?" I heard Dad ask, his question muffled by the sound of numerous eighteen-wheelers idling all around us. He looked at the car, obviously expecting me to get out and switch cars for the drive back to Albuquerque.

"Danny," Porky said solemnly, "Kim's in bad shape. He can't get out of the car on his own."

When Porky opened the door, the icy wind whipped right through the blanket. My father's eyes met mine before glancing at my cut-up face, ripped ear, and mutilated nose. He shivered, and I knew it wasn't from the cold.

The two of them got me switched to Dad's car, and we took off for Albuquerque, a customary hour-long drive. But this wasn't the customary trip. By the time we hit the on-ramp to the interstate, Dad was going 110 miles per hour.

For the third time in twelve hours I found myself trying to find a comfortable position in the passenger seat of a car. Nothing seemed to help. I was gurgling more with every breath, unable to get enough air. Inhaling deeply had gone from painful to impossible.

We zoomed along the interstate at two miles a minute, in and out of freezing rain. Through it all there were times when I thought I would never take another breath. The broken ribs had damaged my lung, and I felt as if I was slowly slipping away.

There wasn't much conversation during that trip. Every once in a while Dad would say, "Are you all right, son?"

My internal response was always, *No, I'm not all right. My wife is dying, and I might be dying too. We've only been married ten weeks, and now it's all going to be over in a matter of hours . . . if it's not over already.* But all I could say was, "Just get me to Albuquerque, Dad."

Every few minutes Dad called Mom at the hospital to see how things were going. After every call I asked him if there was any news.

"They're still working on her," was the only answer I ever got. I didn't know until later then when Dad had still been in Roswell, he had called the hospital and was told that Krickitt probably wouldn't make it through the night.

I was under no illusions that Dad was telling me everything he knew about Krickitt. I had seen her on the gurney in Gallup. I had heard the ER doctors and nurses talking. They had brought me her wedding ring and acted as if it was already over. It seemed to me they had given up on my wife before they even loaded her into the helicopter.

Even as we approached Albuquerque, I believed in my heart that Krickitt was dead. When I had told that nurse that if Krickitt died I didn't want to live, I had truly meant it. I lay there thinking, *I can end my agony right here, right now. All I have to do is just reach up, yank on the door handle, and roll out. At over 100 miles an hour there's no doubt what the result would be.* But as soon as I had that thought, I felt a strong, peaceful presence in the car with me that could only have been God's Spirit. A voice said, "Wait a minute." I don't know if I audibly heard the words or just felt them, but they were there, and they saved me from the most horribly selfish decision I ever could have made. I don't know if I ever actually reached for the door handle or not, but I know I never considered taking my own life again. Even to this day I feel ashamed of those thoughts as I see our two loving children. Taking my own life would have denied them theirs.

At last we came over a rise and saw the city of Albuquerque spread out below us. I propped myself up on the seat and looked down at the city. I wondered where my wife was in that huge sea of lights.

When we were five blocks from the University of New Mexico Hospital, Dad called the hospital emergency room and told them to be ready for me when we arrived. It had been ten hours since the accident, and I still hadn't received much more than basic first aid. By the time we rounded the last corner and pulled up to the emergency entrance, a crowd was waiting — doctors, nurses . . . and Mom. I took her presence as a bad sign.

Someone opened the car door and I tried to get out of the car on my own. Mom looked at me with concern, and I watched as her expression turned first to shock and then to horror at the sight of my disfigured face. Then she disappeared from my line of vision, crowded out by orderlies and doctors huddling around to help me out of the car. They were talking to me and to one another so fast I didn't know what was going on.

"Where's Krickitt? Where's my wife?" I shouted above the noise as loud as I could. It seemed as if no one was listening. "Somebody please tell me what's happened to my wife!"

All of a sudden a familiar voice broke through the chaos. "Coming through! Out of the way!" It was Mike Kloeppel, my best man from our wedding, another bear of a man who was coming to my aid just as Porky Abeda had. Mike knew my first priority was to find out about Krickitt, not for the medical staff to take care of me. I soon saw him come barreling through the mob to tell me about my wife, pulling nurses and other ER staff away as he came. I saw someone grab him by the shirt, but he easily shrugged the hand off.

When Mike got close enough to be sure I could hear him, he asked me, "How are you doing, bud?" Ignoring his question, and fearful to hear his response to my own, I asked him, "Mike, is she still alive?" Mike paused with a sigh and said, "She's still hanging in there, Kim. They're still working on her in the ICU." I felt relief flood through me as I sent up a silent prayer of thanks on that Thanksgiving morning.

Once Mike was out of the way, I was rushed into the emergency room. After the doctors got a good look at my injuries, they couldn't believe I had been released from the hospital in Gallup in the shape I was in. I didn't have the strength to explain that I had released myself against medical advice.

The same physicians who had worked on Krickitt when she had arrived came to check me out and started ordering IVs, X-rays, and CT scans. Nurses scattered in every direction to carry out their demands. I learned that due to the knot they had discovered behind my injured ear, they thought I might have brain swelling and permanent damage.

One of the doctors asked me where I hurt. "My back," I said. "I can hardly move without pains shooting all the way up and down it." They rolled me over to check it out. I heard somebody exclaim, "Look at that!" Apparently, as the car had skidded upside down on the pavement, slivers of glass from the car's sunroof had been wedged into my back. A couple of them were four inches long.

The doctor pulled a curtain around me in an attempt to shield me from his rage, but I could still hear him asking anyone within earshot, "Did he even get any treatment in Gallup?" Of course, he didn't know the whole story. I had been more than happy for the hospital staff at Gallup to give their undivided attention to my wife, and it had kept her alive.

I later learned that the nurses on Krickitt's lifesaving flight confirmed the quality of care she had received in Gallup, writing, "The major credit for your recovery goes to the Gallup EMTs at the scene and Drs. Kennedy and Beamsley at Rehoboth Hospital. They did all the right things. We just flew as fast as we could." It was in no way the Gallup hospital staff's fault that I had demanded to be released in the condition I was in.

While the doctors worked on me, I kept asking Mom how Krickitt was doing. During those physically agonizing minutes and hours the only thing I wanted was for my mother to relieve my emotional and mental agony by telling me that my wife was going to be all right. She wouldn't say it. She couldn't say it. What she was keeping from me was that none of the helicopter team expected her to survive. The admitting physician in Albuquerque had given her less than a 1 percent chance of making it. Krickitt's only hope was a miracle.

Soon my twin brother, Kirk, arrived from Farmington, our hometown in northwestern New Mexico. He and his wife hadn't gotten the news until after midnight, but they came as soon as they could.

"How you doing, Kimbo?" he asked, doing his best to smile.

"I've been better," I answered. "I need to see Krickitt."

"You will," he said. "Just hold on until they're ready for you."

Meanwhile, the ER team got my nose put back in the right place, set my broken hand, worked on my ribs, gave me a sedative, and got ready to admit me to the hospital. Since they were done working on me, I told them I wanted to see my wife as soon as possible.

"After you're admitted, you won't be able to go see your wife," someone explained.

"Then you're not admitting me."

They understandably tried to argue with me, but I wouldn't listen. I refused to be admitted before I saw my wife.

They finally agreed to send me to the recovery room to monitor me and said that if I showed some stability I would be allowed to go see Krickitt. She was still in the ICU, and I was told they would take me there in a wheelchair. They warned me about what I was going to see. I was told to prepare myself for a huge shock when I saw the extent of her injuries and the vast amount of machines in her room. But that didn't matter to me. I was just glad she was still alive.

When we got to the door to the ICU, I motioned for the orderly pushing my wheelchair to stop. "If there's a chance she can see me, I want her to see me walking. I'm going in under my own power," I explained. Then I struggled out of the wheelchair and shuffled through the doorway.

I was grateful the orderly was right behind me with that wheelchair as I stepped forward, because as soon as I saw Krickitt I fell right back into it. Amazingly, she hadn't needed surgery, but because of her brain injury she had every possible life support machine hooked up to her. She was tied down to the table, and she was straining against the straps and flailing around with seizures. Her eyes and lips were still deep purple. Her entire body was swollen like a balloon, and her head was the size of a basketball. I could see some tubes going into her mouth and nose and others disappearing under the sheets, and there were IV lines going into both arms and one foot. There was a probe called a camino bolt drilled into her head to measure the pressure between the brain and the skull, with wires coming out of her head and connecting to some of the monitors that literally filled the room.

She was sedated and couldn't talk because of all the tubes, but I was desperate to receive some kind of communication from her. I got up out of the wheelchair again and grabbed my wife's hand.

"It's me, babe," I said softly. "If you can hear me, squeeze my hand." Due to the plethora of other, more urgent injuries, we didn't yet know that the cool, white hand I held so gingerly was broken. I saw no reaction on her face after I spoke to her . . . but she squeezed.

A flicker of hope flared up inside me. Krickitt was still in there. Somewhere under all those wires and tubes my wife still lived. It was the first sign of life that we didn't need a machine to measure. While it was seemingly just a small thing, I was ecstatic.

The doctors weren't as excited as I was by Krickitt's response. From their point of view, it was still much more likely that she would die than live.

It wasn't long before Krickitt's parents and her brother Jamey arrived from Phoenix. Like many others, they had spent the agonizing hours of the previous night crying and praying for a miracle. But once they arrived, Gus and Mary Pappas were incredibly calm, even at the sight of their daughter covered with tubes and wires, her face distorted almost beyond recognition.

Finally my brother Kelly arrived. He had been level-headed enough to wait until after sunrise to make the trip from Roswell when the roads had thawed. The family circle was complete.

As is usually the case, the visiting hours in the intensive care recovery area were strictly limited. Only immediate family members were supposed to be allowed, and only for thirty minutes at a time. Yet the doctors let us all come and go whenever we wanted to. If any of us had been thinking clearly, we would have wondered why. What we didn't know was that Krickitt's doctors had told the staff to let anybody in at any time, since she would be dead within hours.

The doctors spent a lot of time that day explaining Krickitt's situation to us. We learned that there were two major problems, one of which made the other more serious. The first and most dangerous issue was the swelling in her brain. This swelling constricted the flow of blood to her brain cells, and they were starved for the nutrients and oxygen that the blood normally brought in.

The second concern was that her blood pressure was dangerously low. Even without any other complications, low pressure would have reduced the blood flow to the organs, especially the brain, eventually resulting in damage due to a lack of oxygen. The bottom line was that swelling plus low blood pressure was a double whammy. We didn't need anyone to explain that constricted blood vessels and weak blood flow are a deadly combination.

Because Krickitt had lived this long already, the doctors were actually beginning to think she might survive after all, despite so much evidence to the contrary. Earlier in the morning we had gotten a sign she wasn't paralyzed when she had wiggled her fingers and toes. Still, the doctors said, every minute the brain had insufficient oxygen increased the chances she would have permanent brain damage. The pressure on her brain had gone down for a while, but then it spiked up again without warning. They estimated it would take between twenty-four and forty-eight hours for the swelling to go back down and the oxygen supply to be completely restored. By that time, if she were still alive, my wife would be in a permanent vegetative state.

We had learned how to read the various

monitors in the room, and we spent the next part of the day watching the numbers go up and down. Though we knew what they meant, we were helpless to do anything for Krickitt. Mere numbers on a screen were the indicators of life and death, and there was absolutely nothing any of us could do but sit and watch them change, hoping they would move in the right direction.

Due to all the stress and drama of the past twenty-four hours, it took us a while to remember that we weren't really helpless at all. We had forgotten that God's miracles are a prayer away. We all knew that prayers aren't always answered the way we want, but we hadn't even made an effort to ask God for what we wanted in an organized way.

Soon Jamey, Mary and Gus, Curtis and Wendy Jones, a few other friends, and I found the hospital's chapel. Jamey, who worked with Campus Crusade for Christ at the University of California at Irvine, began the impromptu prayer service. "God, you've said that if we come to you in prayer, you would hear us and grant our request. We ask you to touch Krickitt with your healing hand so that the pressure on her brain will go down . . ." We prayed specifically for the pressure on Krickitt's brain to go down. We prayed for a miracle, asking God to relieve the pressure in time to save her.

It turned out that others were praying for Krickitt too. Her friend Lisa contacted old college friends and coworkers in California and asked them to spend their Thanksgiving in prayer for their friend. Jamey's wife Gretchen, who was expecting a baby and was unable to be with us under her doctor's orders, called a network of Campus Crusade staffers and asked them to pray for a healing miracle. Those people called others, who called others, and by the end of the day people as far away as Russia were praying for Krickitt.

We prayed for about twenty minutes, and then we went back to the ICU. My eyes automatically went to the readouts on the monitors we had been watching for so long. The numbers were better. The pressure on Krickitt's brain was going down, and it just kept going. Nurses were in and out of the room every few minutes, and finally a nurse called for a doctor because she was afraid the monitor probe had slipped out of place. She didn't think the numbers she saw could be accurate. The doctor checked the probe, but it was fine. However, even though the pressure on Krickitt's brain continued to lessen, her blood pressure was still critically low.

People had been calling and visiting all day, wanting to see how Krickitt was doing. Not long after we returned from the chapel our pastor, Fred Maldonado, arrived. We told him what had been happening, and he led all of us to the chapel again to pray that Krickitt's blood pressure would go up.

When we got back to Krickitt's room, we saw that her blood pressure was on a steady rise. When a nurse came in and saw the new blood pressure reading, her jaw dropped. She looked at me and pointed to the read-out. She was speechless for a moment.

"Look at that pressure," she said finally. We *were* looking. It was impossible to take our eyes off of it. It was headed straight toward the normal range.

As the hours passed, Krickitt gradually became more alert. Her vital signs were approaching normal, and it became clear that she was going to get at least some of her basic functions back.

Over the next few days I did my best to rest up and get some of my own strength back. I couldn't yet stand up straight due to the injuries to my ribs and back, but several times a day I would slowly make my way to Krickitt's room. She continued to improve, and on the Monday after Thanksgiving, five days after the accident, she was moved from the ICU to acute care and taken off life support.

Even though Krickitt was fairly alert on rare occasions, she was technically still in a coma. Among the many things I learned during those days, I was surprised to discover that there are fifteen separate levels of coma on the scale they had her classified on, and the least serious ones include states where the patient is actually alert enough to move around and talk a little. That was the case with Krickitt. She slept most of the day, but since the life support tubes had been removed from her throat, I knew there was a possibility that she might talk. I had been desperate for the sound of her voice ever since I had screamed for her in the seconds after the wreck. There had been so many times when I had thought I would never hear it again. I had even been having dreams that she was talking to me, I wanted to hear her voice so badly.

With the doctor's permission, I was feeding Krickitt some ice chips. When I touched a small piece to her lips, she would eat it from my fingers. Her lips weren't so purple anymore. They were very pale and dry, but I could feel their warmth and the whisper of her breath on my skin.

After feeding Krickitt a few chips, I put

my face inches from hers.

"I love you, Krickitt," I said softly.

"I love you too."

I couldn't believe it! My wife had not only spoken, but she had said the words I had most wanted to hear. My Krickitt was back. Just hearing those words made me know things would be fine.

4
LESSON IN HEARTBREAK

The doctors thought Krickitt's declaration of love to me was just a reflexive response. They claimed she likely didn't understand what either of us was saying; her brain just knew that "I love you too" was the default response to "I love you." From a medical standpoint I knew that was true. But for a man who was desperate to get his wife back, those words gave me hope. They were yet another step on the road back for us, even though there was still no way to know how fully she would recover.

In the rare instances when Krickitt's eyes were open, they were frozen in a doll-like stare. She looked at things without any flicker of recognition, and it was obvious she had no idea what was going on. Part of the short-term solution for her recovery ended up being very simple. After wondering about her lack of focus, her dad suddenly realized that she probably couldn't see well. Her contacts had been taken out after the wreck, and nobody had thought to put her glasses on her. Once we did, we saw an immediate difference. She was a lot more aware of her surroundings during the moments she was awake. The first thing she focused on was a plate of Jell-O across the room, and it caused her to became more animated than she had been up to that point. I was overjoyed when she began to focus more on me when I talked to her. It was a tiny victory that moved us closer to the day when I would have my Krickitt back.

Krickitt soon started sitting up, then standing, then taking a few shuffling steps across the room and back with me on one side and an attendant on the other. However, even with the help, she was barely able to lift her feet off the floor. Her right foot was dragging and her wrist was curled up. It was obvious she had neurological damage. It was difficult to watch such an accomplished gymnast struggle so much just to put one foot in front of the other. But the fact that she could move at all was a sign that she would likely regain her balance and coordination enough so that she could walk on her own again one day. She knew how to walk; she just wasn't strong enough to do it yet.

As Krickitt painstakingly took tiny steps, I would encourage her. When I spoke she would look at me. "I love you, Krickitt," I would say as I looked into her eyes.

"I love you too," she said time and again with no vocal inflection or facial expression. I kept hoping to see or hear my old Krickitt, but she wasn't there yet.

It wasn't long before she was allowed to eat pudding and other soft foods. As she was unable to feed herself at that point, I would feed her while she sat propped up in the bed. Sometimes she would look at me or at the food, but much of the time she simply stared straight ahead at the wall.

The next step for Krickitt would be a rehabilitation program. Krickitt's doctors had been discussing the options of where we could take her for the long process of getting her body and mind back to where it had been before the wreck, or at least as close to it as possible. Restoring people with brain injuries to their maximum potential is an intense, highly specialized, expensive process, and the doctors wanted to make sure they sent Krickitt to the best place for someone with her injuries. The good news was that one of the best possible places, Barrow Neurological Institute, was at St. Joseph's Hospital in Phoenix. Since Krickitt's parents lived in Phoenix, this was an optimal choice. But this good news was tempered with some possible bad news. We were told it was not likely our health insurance provider would allow Krickitt to be moved out of New Mexico for her rehabilitation.

As any husband would be, I was incensed that my wife wasn't going to get the best possible care due to what I considered to be a ridiculous health care regulation. "Fine," I said. "Then they can pay for me and for her parents to move to Albuquerque, and they can pay our rent while we're there." Our social worker must have been a lot more diplomatic with the insurance company than I was, because in spite of the dire predictions, our insurance carrier quickly gave us permission to go out of state.

Unfortunately, we soon discovered we weren't going to be able to get Krickitt into the program at Barrow. Instead, arrangements were made for her to be admitted to a head injury rehab program called Rehab Without Walls in Mesa, Arizona. Some doctors who had previously worked at Barrow had started the program, so we knew it would be good, but it wasn't what we had hoped and prayed for. Nevertheless, ten days after the accident, I boarded an air ambulance bound for Mesa with my wife and two medical attendants.

When we arrived in Mesa, the ambulance driver who met us at the plane asked us why we'd landed there since it was an hour away from the hospital. He explained that his instructions had been to take us to Barrow in Phoenix. We explained that we landed in Mesa because we were going to Rehab Without Walls. After several phone calls we finally discovered that while we were in the air, somebody realized that Rehab Without Walls was not an appropriate place for Krickitt. First of all, it was an outpatient facility and Krickitt still needed inpatient care. Furthermore, it was designed for patients who were either a lot further along in their recovery or not as seriously injured as Krickitt was. Once the issue was discovered, Rehab Without Walls had called Barrow and explained that Krickitt was already on her way to Arizona and needed their higher degree of specialized care. The staff at Barrow understood the situation and admitted her immediately.

We arrived at Barrow Neurological Institute late that afternoon, where we soon met the head neuropsychologist. We had brought all kinds of X-rays, CAT scans, and other reports with us, but the doctor explained that they did all their own tests, which they would begin immediately.

After Krickitt's battery of tests, we got her settled into her room. It wasn't long until another doctor came in to introduce himself. He introduced himself as Dr. Singh's associate. Dr. Singh would be Krickitt's doctor, the associate explained, and he would meet her for the first time the following Monday morning. Since it was Friday we would have the weekend to get used to the surroundings before Krickitt started her therapy on Monday. While a rehabilitation center was the last place I would have ever imagined I would be mere months after my wedding, I felt good about where we were. It was obvious God had been working behind the scenes to get Krickitt to the place where she would get the best possible care.

Though Barrow was a specialized hospital, the rooms were the typical hospital fare: plain furniture and yellowish-tan walls. Krickitt's room was directly below the heliport, so we were often disturbed by the sounds of helicopters coming and going. She also had the distinction of being next door to a woman we nicknamed Moaning Lady because she would moan for hours at a time. But despite the noise above and around us, we also had snippets of peace. Krickitt's room had a window facing a courtyard that was full of flowerbeds and walkways. Nothing was blooming in the first week of December, but I still looked forward to the possibility of someday taking walks out there with Krickitt by my side. She had already come so far, and she was under the best possible care. I imagined it wouldn't be long before we were out there looking at the flowers and talking about going home to our apartment and life in New Mexico.

During Krickitt's time at Barrow, I had the opportunity to meet some of the other patients in the rooms around hers. They were all at various stages in their recovery, and it was good to see the progress the others were making. It gave me hope for Krickitt. Some of the other patients had been in car accidents like she had, while others had suffered strokes or aneurysms.

On Krickitt's first full day, a nurse and I took Krickitt out for her first look at another part of the hospital. We wheeled her into the patient cafeteria for lunch. However, Krickitt wasn't prepared to see others with debilitating neurological conditions. I could sense her fear as soon as we entered the room. "This scares you," I said almost involuntarily, not exactly sure if I'd said it out loud or just thought it.

"Yeah," Krickitt answered, her voice still a little raspy after five days with a breathing tube down her throat. I was amazed the scene had penetrated even her hazy consciousness. I hadn't expected her to respond to me, and I felt a burst of joy in spite of the stress I knew she was experiencing. We went back to the room, and Krickitt ate her meals there until she could go to the regular cafeteria. Our doctor heartily approved of this plan, as he did not want Krickitt to be constantly reminded of the possible negative, permanent effects for people with head injuries. Instead he — and I — wanted her to regain her strength and focus on getting better every day.

Though she had such a negative reaction to the cafeteria, the taste of food was actually one of the few pleasures Krickitt could appreciate. Mealtime became a treat for both of us. She simply enjoyed eating. And I loved meals because they were the few times in the day when Krickitt was the most animated. It wasn't long before she was eating on her own. While we spent this time together, she began talking more and seemed a little more connected to me during our conversations.

■ ■ ■ ■

During that first weekend at Barrow we learned about Krickitt's daily schedule. She would start the day with occupational therapy, where she would relearn personal skills like getting bathed and dressed. Next, she would spend time with a speech therapist who would identify any speech disability caused by the injury and teach Krickitt how to overcome it. Her third session of the day would be physical therapy. During this time she would work on her hand-eye coordination, balance, and motor skills. Finally, she would get a break for lunch. Then she would spend the afternoons working on basic household chores such as cooking, vacuuming, and making a bed.

It was hard to believe that Krickitt would soon have such a packed schedule. After all, she was still technically in a coma. In fact, she wouldn't be considered to be out of her "charted coma" until months after the accident. When we first arrived at Barrow, less than two weeks after the accident, she was only awake a few hours a day and she was extremely disoriented. The first night at Barrow she woke up, tried to get to the bathroom by herself, and ended up getting stuck in the bed rail that had been raised for her protection. From then on, someone slept in the room with her every night. This task usually fell to her mother, since I was still not in good physical shape due to my own injuries.

Since Krickitt was still sleeping more than twenty hours a day and couldn't carry on a conversation for more than a minute or two, I wasn't sure how her first official day of therapy would go. On that first Monday morning after we arrived, the day she was scheduled to meet Dr. Singh, I got to Krickitt's room early because I had a plan for getting her ready. My intention was to try and wake her gently and then help her prepare for the big day ahead. I tried talking to her and stroking her face, but I got no response. Then I shook her shoulder, but still she didn't so much as twitch.

At that moment Dr. Raj Singh entered, dressed like he'd just stepped out of *GQ* magazine. He was nothing like what I had expected — no white lab coat, no stethoscope, no clinical aloofness. He gave me a reassuring handshake, approached the head of the bed, and leaned over Krickitt. I had been doing my best to bring her to consciousness carefully, but the doctor had a different plan.

"You have to wake up," Dr. Singh said firmly. Again, Krickitt didn't respond.

"You have to wake up," he repeated with exactly the same inflection. Still nothing.

Then Dr. Singh did something I wouldn't have dreamed of doing. He reached over and gave Krickitt a hard pinch inside the front collar of her hospital gown. Her eyes flew open and she shouted, "Leave me alone!" along with a choice curse word. I was shocked to hear such language coming out of my wife's mouth.

However, the strategy worked, because Dr. Singh now had Krickitt's undivided attention. He told her to wiggle her right hand. She did. He told her to wiggle her left foot, and she did. Dr. Singh shot me a huge grin. "She will do well," he said confidently. Within the hour Krickitt had begun her first occupational therapy lesson.

At times it was hard for me to remember that Krickitt wasn't the only person who had been injured in the accident — I had been too. While we were in Gallup and Albuquerque, I had been in and out of the hospital as a patient a total of six times, yet I'd never been formally admitted overnight because I couldn't stand to be away from Krickitt. I thought about her every minute of every day. I was terrified that she would die when I was away, even though she was continuing to improve a little bit at a time. Even when I did manage to catch a few minutes of sleep, I was never truly able to relax because I was so worried about her.

However, my broken bones were on the mend, and the surgeons in Albuquerque had repaired my ear and nose. Amazingly enough, in a few months no one would be able to tell I had ever injured them. But my back was another story. I was in constant pain. Though the cuts from the sunroof glass were healing, I had searing nerve pains shooting up and down my spine. I never knew when they would come or how long they would last. I was taking strong painkillers just to get me through each day.

When I thought about what we had been through, I was still amazed that our lives had been spared. My mom and dad had gone to the wrecking yard in Gallup to see if they could find my wallet in what was left of our car. Our brand new Escort was completely crushed, and the inside was covered with bloodstains and hair. It looked as if no one could have survived the accident, but amazingly all three of us did.

Once Krickitt was on the road to recovery, I was able to turn a little bit of my focus to filing insurance claims and organizing the medical paperwork that was already starting to stack up. During our first days at Barrow, when Krickitt was still in a coma, we had gotten a call from one of the emergency equipment providers. Much to my dismay, they already wanted to know when they might expect their check. I hadn't realized the financial pressure would begin so soon.

In the midst of all the stress and uncertainty, I was beginning to wonder if I could keep it all together. My wife had an unknown level of brain damage, I was in a state of constant pain and worry, and I was already being pressured to start paying the astronomical medical bills. How was I going to cope?

At times I would momentarily forget about the enormity of the situation while I remembered the few happy moments or funny things that had happened over the past three weeks. But then I would start thinking of Krickitt lying in the dark in her hospital bed. I would imagine her there asleep, taking one slow breath after another. Would one of those breaths be her last? I knew she was getting better, but what if she had a setback? What if the doctors hadn't discovered some major injury that could kill her in a heartbeat?

Then I would wonder what my wife would be like when her rehabilitation course was finished. We hadn't even been married three months — less than one season. We'd had a fantastic wedding ceremony and Hawaiian honeymoon. Then we'd moved into our apartment in New Mexico, unpacked, and started our jobs. That was it — the sum total of our married life. *Will Krickitt ever be the same person as the woman I married?* I wondered. *Will she recover enough to have a career? Will she be able to have children?*

All these thoughts tumbled around in my head night after night as the darkness turned to gray and finally the colors of the day would appear. Then I would get up, get dressed, and head out for another day at Barrow.

I intended to stay in Phoenix for the duration of Krickitt's rehabilitation, so I had moved in with Krickitt's parents once we arrived in Arizona. I had no idea how long I would be there. During those first couple of weeks I hardly thought about my job or any of our responsibilities back home in Las Vegas.

Gilbert Sanchez, the president of New Mexico Highlands University, had tried to call me at the hospital in Albuquerque when

I was still in the ER. He was finally able to connect with me soon after we got to Phoenix. I told him what I could about our situation. There was still so much we didn't know, though, and I explained that I had no idea when I'd be able to get back to New Mexico and my job. After Christmas vacation my team would need to start working out and getting in shape, and there were other athletic department responsibilities I — or someone — needed to deal with. I knew I should have been in touch with someone at the university to tell them what was happening and to work on finding someone to take my place while I was gone, but I just hadn't had the time or the energy to do it. I had more or less deserted my team and my bosses in the midst of my tragedy.

Gilbert was characteristically generous and matter-of-fact. "Take all the time you need," he told me on the phone. "You'll always have a job. We'll get whatever help we need for the department until you get back." He also made me promise to give him weekly updates on Krickitt's condition.

Our friends back at Highlands were already helping us in other ways too, without us even asking. My friend Mike collected our mail and sent it on to me in Phoenix.

Some cheerleaders had temporarily moved in to our apartment to take care of things there. And when our landlord heard what happened, he told me not to worry about the rent. If we could pay him later, that was fine, but if not we should just forget about it. I was stunned by his generosity and grace.

Some of Krickitt's friends had come to visit her while we were still in Albuquerque. After she was moved to Phoenix, other old friends came to visit and decorated her hospital room with Christmas lights and a little tree.

Krickitt's two former roommates, Lisa and Megan, weren't able to visit from California until after Krickitt was moved to Phoenix. By the time Lisa and Megan came, Krickitt looked much better than she had in the Albuquerque ICU, but she still didn't look anything like her normal self. However, because she had improved so much since the wreck, and since I saw her every day, it didn't occur to me that somebody who hadn't seen her since the wreck might be shocked by her appearance. Therefore, I hadn't said anything to prepare Lisa and Megan for the sight of Krickitt with her partially shaved head, her doll-like stare, and the general look of a person who has been in a coma for three weeks. When they arrived, Lisa eagerly rushed into the room to see her friend. She took one good, long look at Krickitt and started trembling. She opened her mouth but was unable to speak. I quickly escorted her to a private family meeting room down the hall. We spent several minutes there, crying together, before Lisa was ready to return to Krickitt's room.

Like all the thoughtful friends who came to see us, Lisa and Megan were almost like visitors from another planet. They were from a world where people got up, ate breakfast, went to work, watched TV, ate in restaurants, read magazines, took care of the yard, and did all the other normal, everyday things of life without even thinking about them. My world had become a world of doctors, hospitals, hospital food, therapy, living with my in-laws, dealing with collection agencies and medical bills, making calls to our insurance company, and spending as much time as I could with Krickitt. My job, my team, my friends, my married life — it was all like a distant dream.

After only a short time in therapy, Krickitt was obviously improving. Each morning she seemed stronger, more alert, and more talkative. The disturbing stare was nearly gone and she was beginning to interact more naturally in conversations.

The therapists were still being very careful with her, though. They had her move slowly, walk with a harness, and work simple puzzles. Once she could understand conversations and answer questions, the doctors started assessing her memory and other mental skills. At first she sounded like a little girl when she responded to questions. She would speak in a few one- and two-syllable words after long pauses. She had to concentrate hard on what she would say, shaping the words slowly and carefully as though they felt unfamiliar. Yet she improved every day.

I wasn't surprised that just a few days after Krickitt started emerging from the lower levels of the coma scale, she wanted to write in her journal. She slowly and painstakingly dictated the words while her friend Julie wrote them down. "Life is very good. Therapy is very confusing at times. I miss the way things used to be with steady Bible study and church meetings, but I know that's the way things are. The Lord is constantly teaching us. I know He has me in His right pocket and I'm very safe there. I love to see Him really work in my life, and

I know He'll use me in His due time."

My wife may have been confused, she may have lost some of her memory, but she still knew her God. She knew he was in control, and she knew he was working in her life and intended to use her to do his work in his time.

Not long after that I was sitting with Krickitt, who was talking with a therapist that was probing carefully for what Krickitt could remember. Her "I love you" had been the first sign that things were slowly moving toward normal. Her words about God were another sign. Now I was ready for even bigger proof. I wanted my wife back.

"Krickitt," her therapist began in a soothing voice, "do you know where you are?"

Krickitt thought for a minute before replying, "Phoenix."

"That's right, Krickitt. Do you know what year it is?"

"1965."

She was born in 1969, I thought, somewhat frantically. *That's just a little setback — nothing to really worry about,* I tried to convince myself

"Who's the president, Krickitt?"

"Nixon."

Well, he was the president when she was born, I justified.

"Krickitt, what's your mother's name?" the therapist continued.

"Mary," she said with no hesitation . . . and no expression. *Now we're getting somewhere. Thank you, God!*

"Excellent, Krickitt. And what's your father's name?"

"Gus."

"That's right. Very good." He paused before continuing, "Krickitt, who's your husband?"

Krickitt looked at me with eyes void of expression. She looked back at the therapist without answering.

"Krickitt, who's your husband?"

Krickitt looked at me again and back at the therapist. I was sure everyone could hear my heart thudding as I waited for my wife's answer in silence and desperation.

"I'm not married."

No! God, please!

The therapist tried again, "No, Krickitt, you are married. Who's your husband?"

She wrinkled her brow. "Todd?" she questioned.

Her old boyfriend from California? Help her remember, God!

"Krickitt, please think. Who's your husband?

"I told you. I'm not married."

97

5
MOVING ALONG

When Krickitt made her declaration of singleness in such a matter-of-fact way, it felt like someone had thrust a knife deeply into my chest. I looked into her eyes, praying for even the slightest hint that she recognized me. She looked back at me with the gaze of a stranger. Until that point I had hope that my wife, at some level, knew I was her husband. After all, I had been with her for most of her waking moments since the accident. She recognized me when I walked through the door, and she answered back when I spoke to her. But I realized she did the same to the medical personnel. To my wife, I was just another person who was helping her recover. It finally hit me that she had absolutely no idea who I was. I staggered out of Krickitt's room and into the hall, hammering the wall with my fist. Even the searing pain in my broken hand — still in a soft cast — couldn't penetrate my rage.

As fierce as my reaction was, it quickly faded. Spent and defeated, I soon walked back into Krickitt's room and stood beside her bed. She looked up at me without anger or curiosity. She just seemed to be waiting for me to speak to her as I always did. I opened my mouth but found I had nothing to say.

Krickitt's neuropsychologist at Barrow, Dr. Kevin Obrien, explained Krickitt's diagnosis to me in the most encouraging way he could. He told me that the accident actually had caused two kinds of amnesia. The first, post-traumatic amnesia, was a temporary confusion about where she was and what was going on around her. For Krickitt, this type of amnesia was already wearing away, and it would soon disappear completely.

The second type of amnesia was more distressing, at least for me. Krickitt also had retrograde amnesia, a permanent loss of short-term memory. We already knew she had regained her memory of people and events from the distant past. She remembered her parents, brother, and sister-in-law. She remembered her old roommate Lisa. She even remembered her old boyfriend Todd, which didn't bring me great joy. But she could remember nothing from the previous year and a half. And what had happened during those months? My wife and I had met, dated, gotten engaged, gotten married, had our honeymoon in Hawaii, and started our life together in Las Vegas. She didn't remember any of it; she didn't even remember anything about the accident.

Over the next few days I prayed a lot about the future — *our* future. Ever since I had watched the EMTs work on Krickitt while she was still strapped upside down in our car, my whole existence had been focused on getting her back. Miraculously, God had saved her life, and I had been impatient to pick up where we left off and build a future together. But that assumed we would be building on a shared past. Suddenly the past was gone. Now I had no idea when, if ever, my wife's memory would return. Yet I knew that no matter what happened, I had made a vow not just before our friends and family, but also before God. I was Krickitt's husband, for better or for worse. And this was just about the worst I could imagine.

As I lay awake each night praying and thinking about how I was going to adapt to this new life, I would be afraid one minute, mad the next, and everlastingly confused.

All kinds of questions flew through my mind. *What will life be like from now on? What kind of person will Krickitt turn out to be? Will she always be different? Is the young woman I married still in there, or is she gone for good? When will we know that her recovery has stopped — that she has improved as much as she is going to?* It was all I thought about. I couldn't sleep, I couldn't relax, and I couldn't get rid of the stress. Though Krickitt still had a chance to recover part of her lost memory, the doctors had told me there were some things she would never remember. The most agonizing question of all was: *Would one of those things be me?* I quickly put that thought from my mind. I couldn't bear to contemplate the fact that my wife might never remember me.

Krickitt soon got into a routine with her therapy, and we saw steady progress in her coordination, walking, speech, and reasoning. Everything was a process, though. For example, when she started walking on her own, she jerked her right foot forward, then dragged the left one on the floor behind her. Gradually the movement got smoother and more natural. Before long she could dress by herself, eat, and take care of all the basic necessities of life.

During those first weeks of rehabilitation, Krickitt didn't seem to mind me being around, but she talked to me like she talked to all the other familiar faces in the rehab center. At first she was cordial, even friendly, but our interactions were without any depth or dimension. They were strictly surface conversations.

Scott Madsen, Krickitt's physical therapist, was an energetic trainer who had a special gift for encouraging his patients to do just a little more every day than they thought they could possibly do. His plan for Krickitt's therapy included time on the treadmill, working with hand weights, and a range of exercises designed to help her get as much flexibility and strength back as possible.

As a coach, I watched Scott's process carefully. I considered that a physical therapist's relationship with his or her patient was similar to my relationship with one of my baseball players. After Scott had been working with Krickitt for a week or two, I felt like she was getting a little bored with the whole process. Frankly, I thought Scott was going too easy on her. I was convinced that Krickitt needed a fairly heavy dose of coaching along with the rehab. In my opinion, she simply wasn't putting enough effort into it. She needed someone to push her a little.

I finally said, "Scott, you're going too easy on her. Krickitt is not your ordinary patient. She is an Academic All-American gymnast. Her body was in top physical shape before the accident. I think you need to push her a little more."

Scott agreed that Krickitt could handle doing more than she was. I was encouraged by his response, but Krickitt was unhappy with the new standards. She pouted and complained because Scott was always wanting more from her; he was never satisfied.

While it was true that Scott was making Krickitt work harder than before, the change in her routine wasn't all that drastic. Even though Scott had agreed with my assessment, he wasn't about to deviate from what he thought was in his patient's interest, no matter what I had said. But you wouldn't know it by talking to Krickitt. She acted as if he was almost torturing her. And as the physical therapy became more intense, Krickitt's spirits took a nosedive.

From the time Krickitt had started talking again, she had acted strangely childlike. This childishness hadn't gone away with therapy; in fact, it seemed to have become a permanent part of her personality. During her therapy sessions she experienced wild mood swings and threw tantrums that would make a preschooler proud. When she was mad at me, she would lash out at me in sudden bursts of temper. Her lack of subtlety and propriety rivaled that of a little girl, and she had no qualms about telling anybody exactly what she thought about them or their suggestions. She thought nothing of using curse words that she would never have dreamed of saying just a month earlier. She was a far cry from the polite, amiable, easy-going Krickitt of the past.

These traits, I learned, were common for someone with Krickitt's injuries. The frontal lobe of her brain had been damaged — the part that controls personality, emotions, and decision-making. Her parietal lobe was also affected, which meant there likely would be permanent changes in her language and mathematical comprehension ability. Not only would her body be different from now on, but so would her personality. Again, until she got to her final recovery plateau, no one knew how much she would improve or to what extent she might return to her pre-accident self.

Though there were some worrying aspects of this new Krickitt's personality, my fears were often offset by the good things about her recovery. As her therapy continued, she kept getting stronger physically. That was encouraging, but what excited me even more was the mental progress she was making. She started having what are called "flash memories" or "snapshot memories." These were mental pictures she would get of a specific moment during the past year, but the problem was that there was nothing to link those memories with anything from her life before or after them. Even so, I put a lot of hope into these flash memories. I knew they could be the key to her remembering our life together if I should happen to be in one of them. One of these still shots was of her sitting outside at a table surrounded by lush tropical plants. That snapshot was from our honeymoon, though unfortunately I wasn't in the frame of her Hawaiian "camera." But I held on to that memory because it was one more link she had with her — our — missing past.

The most encouraging part of Krickitt's recovery was that somehow her faith in God had remained intact. She remembered things about God, church, and the Bible, as was obvious from her first journal entry after the accident and from other comments she had made about what she called "this

Christianity thing." As scrambled as her thinking was, she had praised God and prayed to him shortly after being charted out of a coma. Even so, I still had some fears about whether or not Krickitt's faith would be as strong as it had been. Her brother Jamey calmed some of my fears with these words: "Krickitt's Christianity is in her core, Kim — it's part of her soul. Her soul can't be affected by any injury because it's immortal. Her faith will always be there. It's there now. We've seen it. God has preserved her for some great purpose, and her faith is there to carry her through."

The advice, encouragement, and love I received from Jamey and other members of the family helped me hold things together when I should have been falling apart. As surely as God had saved my wife for some great, unknown purpose, he also had surrounded me with loving, supportive people I could talk to. When you're a guy — and especially when you're a coach — you often feel as if the world expects you to just suck it up and get on with life. But I absolutely could not have made it without my parents, my brothers, and Krickitt's family to share the burden. I would have given up if I'd tried to keep everything inside.

Krickitt and Kristi Pinnick were gymnasts together at Desert Devils Gymnastics Club. Krickitt then went on and received a full gymnastics scholarship at Cal State Fullerton.

My official photo as Coach Kim Carpenter of the Highlands Cowboys. Krickitt said the uniform made me look like a little boy.

With help from her roommates, I sneaked up and surprised Krickitt under this balcony to propose.

Our engagement photo. The matching outfits
recall our first meeting—on the phone discussing
an order for athletic jackets.

Mr. and Mrs. Kim J. Carpenter,
September 18, 1993.

The wedding party. Some of these friends and family would soon play a part in our lives we couldn't possibly have imagined.

Honeymooning on Maui the first time. Krickitt will never remember it; I will never forget it.

What was left of our car after a collision the night before
Thanksgiving 1993. This angle shows the crushed driver
compartment and the sunroof that sliced up my back.

This angle shows where rescue workers cut the roof and door
apart to get Krickitt out. The car landed upside down,
and she hung suspended by her seat belt for more than half an hour.

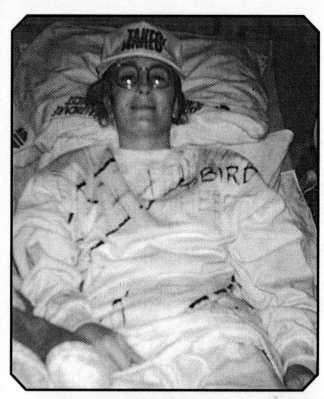

Krickitt at Barrow Neurological Center in Phoenix, Christmas 1993. The fact she was alive was a miracle; at this point we didn't know what level of recovery to expect.

Krickitt, her sister-in-law Gretchen, and brother Jamey at Barrow, January 1994. Jamey and Gretchen were strong spiritual supporters during Krickitt's rehab.

Krickitt with her mom, Mary Pappas, about two months after the accident. Krickitt had graduated to outpatient status.

Krickitt and me in the courtyard at Barrow with my parents, Danny and Mo Carpenter.

Scott Madsen, Krickitt's "physical terrorist," became a real friend who helped me keep my perspective during the inevitable setbacks in her therapy.

Clowning around trying to get reacquainted, February 1994.

Hiking the summer after the accident. Behind the smiles, our relationship was coming apart. Divorce was never an option, but there were times we thought we could never live together again under the same roof.

Krickitt and her family at the North Eastern Regional Hospital rehab center where she worked before the accident, back on the job in the summer of '94. That's Gretchen, Grace, and Jamey up front, with her parents and me in back.

Building new memories.

Getting to know each other again while visiting Krickitt's parents in Phoenix.

Our second wedding ceremony, May 25, 1996, at a remote mountain chapel in New Mexico. It didn't even have electricity, but the view was awesome.

We had agreed to use our original wedding rings in the second ceremony. But each of us secretly bought a second ring for the other, so we had four rings to juggle.

The second wedding party, facing a throng of reporters and photographers from the London *Times, Inside Edition, People* magazine, *Day and Date,* and other media. For keeping our original wedding vows, we'd become celebrities.

At the reception after the second ceremony, three key players in our story: Scott Madsen, Krickitt's physical therapist; Marcy Madsen, recreational therapist; and Bob Grothe, flight nurse.

Krickitt's dad, Gus Pappas, with DJ Coombs, the EMT who overcame her own claustrophobia to climb into our wrecked car and treat Krickitt while she was still trapped inside.

Our second honeymoon in Maui.

In Maui
our second
time around,
strangers rec-
ognized us on
the street, and
a California
radio station
woke us up at
4:00 A.M. for a
live interview.

Backstage in New York with Krickitt's parents and Maury Povich.

Relaxing
in Arizona
at the
Miraval
Resort,
compli-
ments of
*The Leeza
Show.*

Enjoying God's great miracle—a new life together.

Our wedding rings. Special to me (Kim) is my wedding band.
Made from the first wedding ring and a new ring Krickett
gave me for the second wedding. The two were melted
and shaped into one that has the look of both.

Kim and Krickitt arm and arm in the back yard.

Hanging out in the back with the kids, Danny and LeeAnn.

Having some yogurt at the local Aspen Leaf Yogurt Shop.
The family favorite is Cake Batter!

A stroll along the
local Riverwalk
in Farmington,
New Mexico.
Still in love and
always will be!

LeeAnn, Dad,
Mom, and
Danny sitting
on the sand-
stone out the
back gate of
our home.

Hanging out at the Riverwalk in our hometown of Farmington.

The family, football, and the pups Muffin, Joey, Sugar, and Fritzi.

■ ■ ■ ■

Krickitt rang in the new year with consistent, steady progress. We saw a little more improvement every week. Her mood swings were still wild and unpredictable, and she complained regularly about the way Scott was pressuring her to excel in her physical therapy. However, she was stronger and more independent every day. She had started going on short walks with staff members in the neighborhood around Barrow. She loved those outings, especially when she was allowed to go to the nearby shopping center. A near-fatal brain injury had not affected her love of looking for a good deal on shoes.

This might seem like a crazy thing for a husband to say, but I was actually excited about my wife's desire to shop, at least during her rehab days! Because of the shopping option, Krickitt lobbied to go for walks more often, which likely played a part in speeding up her recovery. But as an inpatient, she wasn't allowed to leave the grounds of the hospital by herself.

All of the patients in her area of the hospital wore security bracelets, and every door had a keypad on the wall beside it.

Whenever a patient approached a doorway he or she had to stop until a staff member punched in a code. If anyone wearing a bracelet walked through the door without someone having punched in the code, an alarm would go off.

One day as I was walking down the hall with Krickitt and a nurse, we all stopped short of the door so the nurse could key in the code. But before the nurse could reach the keypad, Krickitt shot her hand out and punched in the numbers. She'd learned the code by watching the nurses. As a result, they had to change the security code for the entire hospital wing. Even though that was a hassle, nobody was upset with Krickitt because it revealed the progress she was making. It was one more encouraging sign of her recovery.

I looked everywhere for indications of the old Krickitt. I just knew that if I could only help her embrace the rehab program with every ounce of her being, I could get her back. I couldn't reach her as a husband, but I thought maybe I could break through to her as a coach. So I traded one identity for the other, coming to her therapy sessions with Scott and pushing them both to pick up the pace. I was like her own personal Jillian Michaels. If Scott told her to do ten sit-ups, I wanted twenty; if he wanted her to walk five minutes on the treadmill, I wanted ten. True to form, Krickitt was not very happy with me in my new role.

A week or two into the new year, Krickitt and I were playing Wiffle ball. I tossed the ball to her underhanded, and she swung and missed time and again.

"Come on, Krick," I prodded, "I know you can hit it. Let's try again."

"I'm tired," she answered with a pout. I could suddenly see what my wife had been like as a six-year old.

"Let's do this a few more times," I encouraged her.

"I don't want to." There was that first grader again.

"Please?" As I said it, I tossed her the ball one more time. Pressing her lips together she gave a mighty swing and connected with the ball. We both watched it sail over the nearby volleyball net.

"That's it, Krick! Way to go!" I was elated.

"You're mean to me."

"Not mean," I answered back. "Just trying to help." For the thousandth time I looked hard for the woman I had fallen so incredibly in love with. I knew she was in that slowly recovering body, struggling to get out. She just had to be. I didn't want to consider the alternative.

The daily therapy sessions became a challenge for Krickitt. It's not that they were physically difficult, she was just bored and distracted most of the time. The only reason she was doing it was because people kept making her do it, not because she wanted to get better. She would do or say anything to get out of doing her therapy. A session would be going along well and she'd stop all of a sudden and say, "I'm tired. I want to go sit down."

"Let's just do a few more reps of this." I wouldn't give in.

"I don't want to! Stop bossing me around! You don't play fair!"

Sometimes she'd be working on movement and coordination in the swimming pool, then quit doing the exercises and suddenly announce, "I'm going to the hot tub."

If I had been in charge of her therapy, Krickitt never would have gotten near a hot tub. Needless to say, I was heavily into tough-love mode. Her parents and the staff at Barrow were a little more understanding. They did what they could to balance out her demands with what they knew she needed. But Krickitt was shameless when it came to pulling people's strings.

One of the few things Krickitt truly enjoyed was food, and her favorite snack was yogurt. We used this knowledge as an incentive to get her to do things she didn't want to do, because we usually could bribe her with a cup of frozen yogurt. However, she was not above putting a big guilt trip on anyone she thought might cave in and give her a treat when she really hadn't earned it. She was rarely successful.

I couldn't seem to build more than a casual friendship with my wife no matter what I did or how hard I tried. When I attempted to play volleyball with her, she quit playing. When we went jogging together, her comments and complaints got steadily more personal and cutting. I never knew what to expect from one day to the next. One minute she'd be friendly and smiling, then I would do or say something she didn't like, and in a heartbeat she would look at me and yell, "Leave me alone! I don't even know who you are!"

One afternoon, still stinging after some sharp rebuke Krickitt had given me earlier in the day, I walked into the physical therapy room and found her lying on her stomach on the carpet, head up, chin resting in the palms of her hands, feet alternately paddling up and down. She was quiet and thoughtful.

"What are you thinking about, Krick?"

She turned her face toward me, still resting her chin on her hands, then turned back. She paused and slowly shook her head.

"Life is so confusing," she said slowly. Then, looking back over at me she inquired, "Are we really married?"

"We're really married, Krickitt. I love you."

Silence followed another slow shake of the head.

Was this our new reality? I could very well be waiting for some kind of recovery or reconnection that never was going to happen. As I walked out of the room I thought, *Is this it? Maybe this is the best it's ever going to be.* For the first time I truly let myself consider the fact that my wife might never be the same person she was before the wreck — the person I fell in love with. Very possibly, the woman I married no longer existed.

We knew that Krickitt's mental recovery could stop suddenly at any point. *What if that happens before she remembers me?* I would think to myself, over and over again. In a way the idea that my wife might never remember me and would never be the same woman I married was harder to deal with than death. If Krickitt had died in the wreck, there would have been a clear ending to our life together. I felt that I could have dealt with that horrible situation because I understood what death was. What I had instead was a complete unknown to me — life in an hazy emotional, spiritual, and relational netherworld where my wife was still with me, but at the same time she wasn't.

At times I wondered how our lives would have turned out if the accident had never happened. I longed and grieved for all the dreams we might now never see come to fruition. But I also came to realize that we had a chance to build a new future together. My wife was still with me. She still could have a life. *We* could still have a life. But I had to accept the fact that it would not be the life I had been looking forward to. As hard as it was, I knew God must have preserved her like this for some great purpose he could see that I couldn't.

When Krickitt had been at Barrow for a month, the doctors started telling us she could soon be released to live with her parents and continue therapy as an outpatient. Krickitt was delighted at the thought, both because she would be spending more time with her family and because she would be spending less time with her physical therapist, who she still thought pushed her too hard.

On January 13, 1994, almost seven weeks after the accident, Krickitt moved into her parents' house in Phoenix. From all appearances she enjoyed being around familiar things: her college yearbooks, photo albums, scrapbooks, furniture she'd grown up with, and mementos from her childhood. Her mom showed her the photographer's proofs of our wedding pictures. They had been sent to Gus and Mary while we were getting settled in Las Vegas, and our plan had been to look at them while we were in Phoenix for Thanksgiving and pick out the ones we wanted to order for our wedding album.

We sat side-by-side on the couch as Krickitt flipped through the photos from our big day. It had all the hallmarks of a traditional wedding — Krickitt in her elaborate wedding gown, me in white tie and tails, the front of the church lit entirely by candles. Her parents and I all hoped that seeing the pictures would spark some more of those flash memories in Krickitt and give her something that might lead back to more detailed memories of our marriage. She recognized the bride in the pictures as herself, but that was all. She still had no emotional connection to me . . . or any interest in creating one.

However, Krickitt did still have an interest in her relationship with God. Soon after she moved home, she told her mother that she had a nagging feeling something was missing in her life. It turned out she missed writing to God in her journal. She had written one lone entry with the help of a friend, but then she forgot about it for a while. Since she had a renewed desire for it, her mom took her shopping for a journal. That seemed to be the answer. Although she was still mentally mixed up much of the time, she had felt the absence of communication with God in her life and wanted to make it a regular part of her routine again by writing to him in her journal. It was a bittersweet feeling for me to know that even though my wife wasn't yet ready to get to know me again, she was ready to draw closer to God.

So the emotional roller coaster continued. One day I'd be riding high because Krickitt had walked farther than ever before on the treadmill, or she had read something she couldn't read the day before, or she had experienced another flash memory. The next day I would drop down into the depths of despair because she had lashed out at me again for pushing her in therapy or because one more potential memory jogger — a picture, a name, a letter, a memento — had failed to bring back any remembrance of our life together.

By the time Krickitt moved into her parents' house, I hadn't worked in two months. My job had been the last thing on my mind. All I had been thinking about day and night was how I could help Krickitt get better. I was still getting no pressure from the administration at Highlands, and the assistant baseball coaches were gearing up for spring training without me there. My parents and in-laws, however, were convinced that the best thing I could do at this point was to get back into my everyday life in New Mexico. They suggested I move back to our apartment in Las Vegas, rejoin my baseball team, and make it a priority to restore some sort of normalcy to life. At first I was totally against leaving Krickitt. But the more I talked about it with all of our parents, the more I agreed it was the right thing to do for both Krickitt and me.

I called Gilbert Sanchez and told him I was ready to come back to work. "We obviously want you back," he said, "but not until you're sure you're ready. Take your time."

"I've taken my time," I answered, "and we're all ready to start getting things back to normal. I want the Highlands Cowboys to get off to a good start this season, and I want to be a part of it."

My stated reasons for going back to work were both valid and true. But I didn't tell President Sanchez the deeper reasons I was returning to Highlands. The main motivating factor behind my return to coaching was that I needed to be around something I could understand and predict and have some semblance of control over. By God's grace I had made it as far as I had with Krickitt, but I sensed it was time to trust him even more. I had gotten to a place where I truly believed that God would work his perfect will with my wife whether I was in Phoenix or Las Vegas. Krickitt had her parents — people she remembered and loved — to take care of her. She didn't need me to be with her twenty-four hours a day. It was time for me to get home and prepare a place for her there.

February 1 was to be my first official day back on campus, but I made one quick trip before that in preparation for my return. While I was there, I kept a fairly low profile

117

since it was a short trip. I would soon be back for good and could see and talk to everyone then. While I was in the locker room at the university, I saw a homemade flyer about a fund drive for Krickitt and me. Obviously, somebody at school had organized an appeal to help us pay our expenses. We hadn't said anything about the astronomical hospital bills, but anyone could have guessed that we were quickly racking them up. I was greatly touched by the generosity of the people of Las Vegas. It was a community where people had very little to give; yet they were willing to sacrifice for us. I didn't know exactly what they were going to do, but I didn't let on that I knew about their efforts.

I went back to Phoenix, said good-bye to Krickitt and her parents, and returned to Las Vegas for good. I was humbled and amazed by my reception. When I arrived at our apartment, I found it freshly cleaned, and there was a hot dinner in the oven. At practice the next day the players and other coaches couldn't have been nicer or more supportive. Even though I had left them without a head coach for more than two months, they weren't upset and they hadn't felt abandoned. They all just wanted Krickitt and me to get better. It was an awesome testament to the value of great friends.

After that first practice, a couple of the players approached me and told me there were some people who wanted to talk to me. I realized the time had come for me to find out what this fund-raising surprise was. I followed the guys around the corner, where a group of friends, community members, and coworkers greeted me.

As I tried my best to act surprised, one of the women stepped forward. "We want you to have this," she said as she handed me a huge jar full of money. I no longer had to act surprised, because I was floored. There was *a lot* of money in that jar. For weeks this group of people had sponsored bake sales and raffles and had solicited donations to raise money so I could fly back to Phoenix to be with Krickitt. There were checks in the jar from people I knew didn't have enough money for their own expenses, let alone mine. There were also monetary gifts from judges and other prominent people in town. Altogether it was enough for ten round-trip flights between Albuquerque and Phoenix.

I quickly set up an ambitious plan to go to Phoenix for a few days every week. Early each Monday morning I drove two hours from our apartment in Las Vegas to the airport in Albuquerque, caught a plane for Phoenix, and stayed with Krickitt through Wednesday night. On Thursday I caught a 5:30 a.m. return flight to Albuquerque, drove two hours back to Las Vegas, and got back in time to prepare for the day's practice with the team in preparation for our games that weekend. I was the bus driver for our away games, which meant that on some Sunday nights I didn't get back to our apartment until well after midnight. Then on Monday morning I started the cycle all over again.

It was soon clear that this plan wasn't going to work long-term. I already wasn't sleeping much due to all the stress and my back trouble, and this new unrealistic schedule gave me even less time to rest.

At the same time, the calls from bill collectors were starting to get out of hand. Krickitt's medical expenses alone were already more than $200,000. On top of that we had my medical bills, the cost of Krickitt's continuing rehab, and other incidentals such as a replacement car for our Escort, all of which pushed the total debt even higher. By that point we knew that it was not going to be a smooth ride with our insurance company. I had gotten in touch with them soon after the accident, but it quickly became obvious we were not going to get the money we needed to satisfy the collection agencies in the amount of time they wanted us to. That meant we were facing the prospect of a lawsuit just to get our insurance carrier to pay the money we thought our premiums already entitled us to. That, in turn, meant hiring lawyers and going even further into debt.

To make things even worse, as much as I looked forward to my visits with Krickitt, her attitude toward me was on a sharp decline. On Monday afternoons I went straight from the airport to Barrow to help her with her therapy. Sometimes she would greet me in a friendly way when I arrived, and sometimes she'd just make a noise in my direction and go on with whatever she was doing.

In my heart I wanted Krickitt to improve so badly, but encouraging her was a risky proposition. As with anything I did during those days, I never knew how she might react. But my time as a coach had taught me that you have to push people to achieve their potential; they're not always going to see how far they can go as well as a coach can. So I pushed Krickitt because I thought it was best for her. However, one little nudge of encouragement might not get any reaction from her, but the next one could set off a flood of anger.

"Quit telling me what to do! Leave me alone!" she would shriek at me.

"I'm only trying to help you get better," I would explain yet again. "You want to get better, right?"

"I hate you! Why don't you just go back to Las Vegas or wherever it is you come from?" my wife would say to me.

"Because I care about our relationship and I love you."

At times, her face frozen in a bitter stare, she would turn away without another word. It seemed to me that these interchanges would never end.

Most Thursdays, on the return flight to Albuquerque, I would be looking down at the desert as the sun came up ahead of me. The faint glow of the sunrise always reminded me of the glow that had filled the church when I watched the woman of my dreams — the woman God had saved for me alone — walk down the candlelit aisle. There, holding each other's hands in front of our families and everyone we loved, we had both made a vow. The woman I loved more than any other had looked steadily into my eyes and proclaimed in a clear, confident voice:

"Finally today is here, the day that I give you my hand in marriage. I'm honored to be your wife. I'm all yours, Kimmer. And I love you."

But she no longer thought she was my wife. She didn't want to be mine. In the disoriented state she was in, she did not know what she wanted. I felt she had no more love for me. Just a few months after our wedding, the woman I had married seemingly hated me. And it was breaking my heart.

6

A NEW REALITY

Regardless of how my wife felt about me, I still loved her. And I was determined to keep the vow I had made to be faithful and to devote myself to her every need. Even though it was exhausting, both physically and emotionally, I continued to make that weekly trip from Las Vegas to Phoenix to be with Krickitt and encourage her during therapy. I had become almost relentless in my pursuit to push her to her physical limits. When I was with her in the physical therapy room, there was no longer any sign of a husband, just a coach.

I knew Krickitt wouldn't appreciate my effort; instead she hated it and often she let me know just that. At times she was quiet and agreeable, but the more I prodded her to push herself, the more she screamed and got upset. She was still acting and reacting like a child and at times was unguarded with her speech.

The doctors had warned me that she could be very uninhibited, and there were times when uninhibited only began to describe her. I had to learn to expect the unexpected. Even with people in the room, she'd sometimes express inappropriate thoughts or grab me without any warning. Then when I would resist she'd say something like, "You don't love me any more. You don't love me because I'm disabled!" I have to admit that part of me wanted the physical part of our relationship back, but it was just too strange emotionally — at that point she was more like a daughter to me than a wife. Oddly enough, later in the day she could be back to declaring she hated me. When it came to Krickitt's emotions, anything could happen at any moment.

Krickitt's doctors thought a visit to our apartment in Las Vegas might jog her memory of me. Her mom flew with her from Phoenix to Albuquerque, and my parents drove in for the big event. We were all hoping against hope that when Krickitt walked into our home, she would suddenly remember everything and return to being the woman she had been before the wreck.

When I got home at the end of the day, Krickitt was friendly. But even though she had just seen me a few days before, she really didn't act as if she had any interest. Her mom said that when they arrived, the two of them walked around the living room, looking at the furniture, the pictures on the walls, and the books in the bookshelf. Mary said Krickitt revealed no emotion whatsoever. As she stood in the middle of the room and looked around, it was obvious that she remembered nothing about it.

Krickitt asked what her china pattern looked like. Her mom handed her a plate. Krickitt lifted it close to her face, then set it down again. "That's nice," she said simply. She had no remembrance of the pattern she had painstakingly chosen after a lot of shopping around and getting advice from her mother and friends.

As I led her on a tour of our apartment, I would ask her questions about different things I thought might ring a bell: pictures of the two of us, furniture we'd picked out together. None of it brought back any memories. My wife was a stranger in our own home.

Krickitt's doctors had suggested we watch the video of our wedding. They hoped it might trigger something in Krickitt's memory about her married life. When I asked her to watch the video with me she agreed. We sat together on the couch and watched the entire ceremony. I could sense that she knew how important it was to me that she remember something — anything — about the event, and she tried to be encouraging. "I recognize that girl — that bride — in the video as me," she said thoughtfully, "but I don't have any connection with her. I don't know what she's thinking and feeling. I see the two of you exchanging vows, but it's like watching a friend on video. I don't know what the girl on the screen is thinking." There was no emotion in her voice as she spoke about our wedding, and I could tell there was no feeling for me in her heart.

A few weeks later I was in Phoenix helping Krickitt with her therapy, as usual. What wasn't usual was that after the session, her physical therapist asked me if I'd like to help him coach a boys' basketball game after he got off work that afternoon. Grateful for a break in the routine, I accepted Scott's invitation.

My time with him was nothing short of a blessing. For two hours I completely forgot about having a wife who didn't know who I was, having a towering stack of medical bills, and being completely exhausted every day and every night of my life. I got completely caught up in the strategy of the game and trying to help Scott's team come out on top.

After the game the two of us went to the snack bar. We debriefed a little about his team's performance, and then he brought me back to reality. "I know you're getting discouraged about Krickitt," he said. "I honestly don't know how you keep going."

He knew the truth of Krickitt's situation — and mine — so I didn't hesitate in opening up to him. "It's tough. Really tough," I admitted. "Sometimes I get so excited when I think we're about to have a breakthrough, when I think she remembers something that would link her life to mine. But then she does or says something hateful because she thinks I'm pushing her too hard in therapy — or for no reason at all — and it tears my heart out. It's the toughest coaching job I've ever had."

"We can keep on helping Krickitt," Scott continued. "Physically she's making incredible progress. If she hadn't been in such good condition because of her gymnastics, she'd never have made it this far. But your well-being is important too. Krickitt needs somebody strong, confident, and forgiving; you've got to be that to her, but you can't do it by yourself. You need God, Kim."

"You're right," I said. "But it's tough to think that way when just getting through the day often seems like an impossible task."

"God hasn't forgotten you," he said with quiet confidence. "God will never forget you. He says he will never leave you comfortless, and he won't. You can't use him up or wear him out. Hang on to him, Kim. He's the most powerful force for good you have. He won't forget you. So please don't forget him."

Lying awake at the Pappas house late that night, I mulled over Scott's advice. Maybe I'd forgotten to take my troubles to God. Perhaps in all the exhaustion and desperation I had overlooked the most powerful tool of all for Krickitt's recovery. It wasn't that I hadn't prayed. I had, and often. But I knew that my focus had been on Krickitt and my desires for her and us, not on God and *his* desires for us. I needed to focus more on him. I needed to trust him more, because he is the one who is all-powerful, not me. So I made God a promise that I would always remember to trust in him and his amazing power.

That evening I thought about that first night in the hospital in Albuquerque when Krickitt's cranial pressure was increasing by the minute and we didn't know whether she would live or die. During the course of those uncertain hours, I had felt myself gradually but steadily trusting God with my wife's life. Scott's advice three months later was like a refresher course in putting my faith in God's ability instead of in my own.

The more I trusted in God's wisdom and power, the more at peace I felt, even though I knew he might take Krickitt away from me at any moment. I was coming to a point where I had hopes of it working out, but I reached the conclusion that it may not. As painful as that thought was, I made a commitment to myself and to God to continue to physically be there for Krickitt until at least the day came when she no longer needed my support and could live on her own. Then I would ask her what she wanted. If her desires did not include me, I would honor her wishes and let her go. I knew I had made a vow until death do us part, but I also knew that I had to keep a real perspective. I often wondered when that day would come. I knew it was a day I would have to face, but I lived in fear of the possible outcome.

From time to time there were tantalizing signs that Krickitt was beginning to accept her new life. One day I was talking to her mom on the phone and she mentioned that Krickitt had told the therapist she "missed that guy who calls and hangs around." I was overjoyed that she remembered my visits and seemed to have a desire to spend time with me, even though she didn't always act like it when I was actually with her.

I did my best to call Krickitt every day I wasn't with her. But one night I didn't call at my usual time. A couple hours later the phone rang, and it scared me. When I answered the phone it was Krickitt's mom. She said, "Kim, there is someone here who wants to talk to you." I was ecstatic. She put Krickitt on the line.

"Hi, this is Krickitt."

"Hi Krick, I'm really glad you called."

More silence. Then, "Well, I gotta go now. Good-bye."

Those were the greatest words I had heard in months. I believed right then that we were going to make it and that Krickitt felt something for me down deep, but she just couldn't put the pieces together on the phone. This was the first of many times she'd call, say a sentence or two, and hang up. But I didn't mind that those conversations were so short. They were just more confirmation that my wife was warming up to me.

A few weeks after that first call from

Krickitt, Mary called with some more encouraging news. Krickitt had been looking in the mirror, focusing on the place where her skull had been dented in the wreck. She touched it as she inspected it, feeling around it with the tips of her fingers.

"Hmmmmm," she said. "Maybe I really did have this accident."

Since Krickitt had first come out of her coma, she had kept telling us she felt like she was in a dream that we were all part of. She insisted there hadn't been a wreck and she had never been married. She believed she was trapped in a nightmare and knew she would eventually wake up. Her reaction in front of the mirror was the first solid indication that she was beginning to realize that her dream world might be real after all.

This realization was a promising sign and an answer to prayer, but Krickitt's next trip to Las Vegas a few weeks later was anticlimactic. She came back to our apartment and looked at everything like she had before. She wasn't as lost or disoriented, but that wasn't because she ever remembered living there with me. She only remembered it from having visited just a few weeks before. So we went through the same motions we had the first time: looking at the china, the wedding pictures, and the wedding video. She seemed to like it just fine, but nothing helped her really connect with her past.

Krickitt's second visit home was the first time there was any coverage of our story in the media. That Friday, the local *Daily Optic* ran a story in the sports section about our upcoming baseball game that weekend. They explained that in my opinion, my wife would be the most important fan in the crowd.

"Before the accident we were caught up in the will to win," they quoted me as saying. "It took something devastating like this to make me realize that winning is not everything. Until you go through something like this, you don't understand. My outlook on life in general has changed. You tend to respect life a lot more. My priorities are a little different." That was an understatement.

Krickitt's mom had traveled to Las Vegas with her again, and when we were at the airport on their way back to Phoenix Mary stepped away from us at the gate so Krickitt and I could have a private moment to say good-bye.

I held her beautiful face in my hands.

"I love you, Krickitt," I said.

"I love you too." Her mouth spoke, but her eyes said nothing. She gave me a quick hug, like one she might give anyone she was fond of. As we embraced, I shot a quick glance at my mother-in-law across the waiting area. I saw the same aching, overwhelming disappointment in her expression that she could no doubt see in mine.

Krickitt finally progressed enough that Dr. Singh and the rest of the team at Barrow set a tentative date for her release from the outpatient program. In spite of her memory loss, Krickitt was excited about getting back to Las Vegas. Though she still lashed out at me without any warning, we were definitely beginning to rebuild our relationship.

On the surface Krickitt was still ambivalent about our relationship. In fact, she didn't always accept me as her husband. But though I didn't know it at the time, deep down and in moments of mental clarity, she knew we were married and she wanted the marriage to work.

Her journal from that time reads, "Dear Lord, . . . I really want to be back with Kimmer and get our new life going again. I am relying on you to restore all of my feelings for our relationship. . . . Thank you for sparing our lives in the accident, and I ask that you would use us for your glory. Please strengthen our marriage and make it even stronger than it was in the beginning. Help us to grow closer together. We give you our trust and thanks. . . . May I become the girl I was and the one you want me to be."

Though I didn't know what was going on in Krickitt's mind or her heart, I did know that she now missed me on the days I didn't call or visit. There were even times when she enjoyed being with me and we really seemed to be getting somewhere. I held tight to those moments and frantically tried to figure out what made them work so I could hopefully try to create them more often.

As Krickitt's release date approached, we both felt the strain of not knowing for sure whether she would be allowed to leave the program and come back to Las Vegas. They took note of her astonishing progress and reported, "She is very eager to return to her husband in New Mexico." Although she had made huge strides in her recovery, she still had some physical limitations. For instance, she couldn't qualify to get her driver's license back yet because she had intermittent vision problems. But in the end everybody signed off on her release, and on April 14, 1994, Krickitt came home.

Four days later we celebrated our seven-month anniversary. At that point Krickitt had spent two-thirds of our married life as a hospital patient, and I had spent two-thirds of our married life wondering if my wife would ever remember that she had, indeed, married me.

Though I had tried to prepare myself for Krickitt's reentry into life in New Mexico, it didn't take long to realize our life together was a disaster in the making. We couldn't relax around each other. Even though she had missed me when I was away, she still didn't always accept the fact that we were married, and she didn't know how to live as part of a married couple.

A few days after she got home, I found her standing in the middle of the kitchen with a confused look on her face. I asked her what she was thinking about.

After taking a minute to formulate the words, she said, "How did I do the wife thing?"

I asked her what she meant.

"You know, the wife thing. Did I cook for you? Did I make you lunch? Did I wave to you when you left in the morning? I don't know what I'm supposed to do. I'm so confused. I know I'm supposed to be married to you. I know I like you and miss you when you're gone." She paused before continuing, "I know you've been so faithful. You're always there when I need you. I know these things. I know them. But I don't know I'm married to you. I wish I did, but I don't."

When I would leave for work in the mornings, I had no choice but to leave Krickitt alone in the apartment. I was worried about the prospect, because I remembered how she had always wanted to leave the hospital in Phoenix and go for a walk. I was afraid that she would go for a walk here and get disoriented.

"Promise me you won't run off and get lost," I said.

"I promise," she answered softly.

Just a day or two later, we got into an argument and before I knew it she was gone. I found her a half mile away. She had found a pay phone and had called her mom.

"You promised me you wouldn't run away," I said firmly when we got back to the apartment.

"I can't promise you anything!" she shouted, then ran into the bedroom and slammed the door.

"Krickitt!" I shouted.

"Go away! I hate you!" she screamed.

Then I heard her dissolve into heaving sobs of frustration and rage. I walked away and waited for her to calm down.

And so it went. We would have sweet times of companionship and rebuilding that were suddenly interrupted by the temper outbursts of an unruly teenager. There would be instances when she completely lost control, quickly followed by periods of fear and confusion about her behavior.

Though things were tumultuous at home, I was relieved that I no longer had to make the weekly commute to Phoenix. Staying in one place gave me the chance to settle back into my coaching duties and concentrate on building a winning team. I needed something successful in my life like I'd never needed it before.

The downside was that there was nowhere I could go to get away from the pressure. Since my home life was such a disaster, I was too tired and stressed to be the coach my team needed and deserved. Krickitt was improving from a medical standpoint, but our relationship was in ruins. We were living together but not living as husband and wife. Our interactions were still more like father and daughter or coach and athlete.

During those days Krickitt would lose her temper over the smallest of issues. She would forget where she put things around the house. She rarely made it through a whole day without breaking something. She tired easily. Since she couldn't yet drive, she got bored with staying at home all the time. When she was talking to me or other people, she would laugh when she meant to cry, and she often interrupted others in mid-sentence to blurt out a long story on a completely unrelated subject.

It was as if I was living with two women inside one body. One was kind and gentle and doing all she could to rebuild our married life. The other was a sullen teenager with a quick temper who didn't care that her words would hurt me.

I knew Krickitt had to still be in physical pain because I was, and she had been injured a lot worse than I had. My back was still giving me trouble, but the physical problems weren't the real problem. I had been diagnosed with post-traumatic stress disorder. That, the doctors said, was one of the main reasons I was always tense and unable to sleep. I was prescribed anti-depressants, painkillers, and heavy-duty sleeping pills just to make it from one day to the next.

As if life at home wasn't tough enough, we

were also inundated with bills, calls from collection agencies, and conversations with our lawyer. From the time the bill collectors had started calling just weeks after the accident, various health-care providers and their collection agencies had kept up a steady stream of phone calls and letters. It turned out that the other driver had no auto owner's insurance, so all the expenses fell to our own insurance company. And they were still not cooperating.

The walls were closing in. I felt powerless to do anything to regain control of my life. It was just too much for me. But it wasn't too much for God. As he had so many times over the previous few months, he came to my rescue.

I wasn't surprised that God showed me what to do, but I was surprised about the messenger he chose for the job: my immediate boss at Highlands, Athletic Director Rob Evers. Rob was not just a coworker, but also a good friend. He had encouraged me to stay with Krickitt in Phoenix during her inpatient program at Barrow and had kept my job open for me even when I had no idea when or if I would be back. He knew about my emotional and physical struggles during the weeks of commuting between Las Vegas and Phoenix, and he now had a front row seat for my battle to effectively coach my baseball team while dealing with my new life.

Several months after Krickitt came home, Rob asked me to come into his office. When I sat down, he looked at me with both compassion and an air of authority and told me he thought I needed counseling.

"Krickitt's the patient, not me," I insisted.

"I'm not worried about Krickitt. She has plenty of doctors and therapists watching her progress. She has had the best therapy possible. Most of all, Kim, she has you to love her and look after her. But who's looking after you?"

"I'm going to be all right," I said. "Things are getting better. Krickitt's coming along, and I'm fine. Really."

Rob was not convinced in the least. "Kim, I've watched you with the team. Nobody questions your commitment to the team and your heart for baseball. But you need help. You need counseling, and you need it now. If you say no, I'm putting you on administrative leave."

I responded with a few choice words in tremendous anger. I began to grow bitter, but ironically I was getting my own dose of tough love.

Rob agreed to give me a few days to think

things over. Deep down I knew he was right; I just didn't want to believe it. I wanted to be strong for everyone who was counting on me. My team needed a coach who could focus and lead them to victory. My wife needed a husband she could trust and who would be there for her. I didn't want to face the fact that I was losing ground on both fronts with every passing minute. On top of it all, the last thing I needed was more medical bills. However, the social worker I was asked to meet with assured me that the school's health insurance would cover my counseling sessions.

In the end, I made the painful decision to resign from my position as baseball coach. At that point I wasn't able to focus on both my job and my wife to the extent they needed, and my commitment to Krickitt was my top priority. After all, I had vowed to be there for her for life, and if it was going to work I knew what had to be done. I hadn't made that promise to my team, but still I felt I let those boys down even though I knew I had no choice.

I knew I made the right decision, and I set out to focus on my new job: taking care of Krickitt. Unfortunately, one of my first efforts to spend some quality time with her backfired. The weekend after I resigned from Highlands, the two of us went to a Cowboys baseball game and watched from the bleachers. During the game a bench-clearing fight broke out on the field. The sight of it confused Krickitt and upset her. It didn't help matters any that the coach of the opposing team told me in no uncertain terms that if I had been on the field doing my job like I should have been, the fight never would have happened. Nevertheless, even though others obviously questioned my decision, I knew it was the right one for me and for Krickitt.

By the time summer rolled around, Krickitt had recovered enough to start working part-time again as an exercise technician at the same hospital fitness center where she'd worked before the accident. This was a great move, because it gave her the opportunity to be in charge of something again and have something in her life that she felt she had some control over. As she took this step, I could see traces of the old Krickitt. She still had her sense of responsibility — she was always prepared for the job and was always on time. It was so good to see my wife amongst the backdrop of her old life, surrounded by fitness equipment, weight machines, and free weights. I was proud of how far she'd come.

At the same time Krickitt was becoming more self-sufficient, our relationship was in a death spiral. Just when I thought our home life couldn't be more erratic and stressful, Krickitt's flashes of hatred toward me got more brutal than ever.

One of my most vivid memories of that time was when we were at a car wash, of all places. While we were standing at the exit waiting for the car to appear, we got into an argument. In only a few seconds we were screaming at each other. Soon Krickitt threw her water bottle at me, and the next thing I knew she was striding down the sidewalk away from me. I still couldn't move very fast, but it only took a couple of minutes for me to catch up with her in a fast-food restaurant, where I again found her crying and talking to her mom on the phone.

On another particularly bad day we were in the middle of a rather animated disagreement when she picked a fork up off the table behind her, whirled around, and threw it. It stuck in the wall beside me.

"Leave me alone! I hate you!" If I had heard those words once, I'd heard them a thousand times, but this time it wasn't Krickitt's words I was worried about, it was her actions.

"Krickitt, get a grip!" I typically tried to respond to her anger calmly, but this time I was furious. If she hadn't taken such bad aim, that fork would have sunk into me instead of the wall.

"Stop treating me like a child!"

"Stop acting like one!"

My wife's eyes were filled with hatred. "Maybe I should just slit my wrist."

That was the last straw. "There's a knife in the kitchen," I informed her, pointing in that direction.

"You think I'm kidding, don't you? Maybe I'll hang myself."

"There's a rope in the truck."

Krickitt bolted outside and slammed the door shut behind her. In the few seconds it took me to yank it back open she had disappeared. I found her, exhausted and crying, hiding behind a car in an apartment parking lot down the street.

I helped her back inside and we sat down in the living room. There was a long silence.

"I miss the old Krickitt," I said at last.

"I miss her too," she answered. I wondered if she even knew who the old Krickitt was.

What I later came to realize is that Krickitt was just as frustrated as I was, she just didn't always have the capability to show it in a rational manner. She knew she wasn't the woman she had once been, and she wanted our marriage to work. I later read in her journal, "Dear Lord, I thank you so much for being by my side and being so faithful to me. I need you now, and daily. I can see that I *cannot* do this on my own strength, but I need you to carry me and help me through each and every day. I pray for [our] marriage. Please be the center of it and help us to treat one another with respect and a lot of love. . . . Help me to return to the parts of Krickitt you liked. Please help me and forgive me with all my frustrations."

It was only a matter of time before well-meaning people started asking me — indirectly but unmistakably — if I would ever consider divorce as an option. "At some point you might just have to let this go," they would say. A social worker told me that when a married person has a debilitating head injury, the odds of divorce are around 80 to 90 percent. Someone pointed out that taking that route would release me from my responsibility for Krickitt's medical bills. It would be an easy way out of a lot of problems.

I had a simple answer for anyone who suggested divorce: "No. It will never happen." It simply was not an option for either of us. It didn't matter whether Krickitt remembered me or not, whether it took every penny I had to take care of her, or even whether we ultimately lived together or apart. The simple truth was that I couldn't see myself going through life without the woman I loved — the woman I had vowed to protect through times of challenge and need.

But at the same time I knew we couldn't continue down the path we were on. The more Krickitt recovered physically the worse I felt, because at the same time she was getting well, we were growing more distant emotionally.

For several months I had been battling an idea that I hadn't wanted to share with anyone. Since Krickitt didn't remember me, I wondered whether my responsibility was really to re-establish our household as husband and wife the way it once was. After all, that might never happen. Instead, I was believing more and more that my job as a husband who truly, selflessly loved his wife might be to help restore her independence to the point where she could live the rest of her life on her own if that's what it took to bring her peace.

7
SECOND CHANCES

A year and a half after our wreck, I had finally resigned myself to the fact that my wife would never be the same person she had been before the accident. There were still moments when I would get tantalizing glimpses of the woman I had married that returned me for a split second to the way things had been. But at the same time those glimpses were also heart-piercing reminders of the life I had lost and was never going to get back.

Krickitt never recovered her memory of our meeting, engagement, marriage, honeymoon, or anything of our life together before the accident. In fact, it turned out that for more than a year she was not even always aware that she had a period of unrecovered memory. She was extremely confused during that time because she didn't always know who I was or why I was there, yet for most of that time she was living with me as my wife.

Imagine what that must have been like for her. The movie *50 First Dates* was still a decade away from being released, but anyone who has now seen the movie can get a glimpse of what life was like for Krickitt some days. Thankfully, unlike the woman in the movie, Krickitt eventually did get to the point where she always remembered that she couldn't remember everything about her life.

During that time, Krickitt was given constant reminders from friends and family that she was indeed married to me, and she watched the video of our wedding and looked at our honeymoon pictures a hundred times. She was slowly realizing that life wasn't a bad dream she would eventually wake up from. What she was experiencing was the new reality. And as much as she rejected me at times when she couldn't remember that there were things she couldn't remember, she always had a sense that I was there as her protector and companion. She knew there was something special about me because I went out of my way to be with her and help her. "I figure if I fell in love with this guy before," she said, "I could do it again."

I continued to be amazed that her spiritual

awareness and trust in God seemed miraculously intact. As her brother, Jamey, had said early in her recovery, she had a rock solid "core of Christianity" that even this terrible experience couldn't damage. Could that faith be combined somehow with her faith in our marriage to close the gap between us or at least keep it from getting any wider? Even though she couldn't remember our wedding, would her faith compel her to keep the vows she had made to me?

One big mystery for me was still what Krickitt was thinking from one minute to the next. Her mood swings were so wide and unpredictable. Frankly, our whole relationship was unpredictable. I didn't know what Krickitt was like any more, and I didn't know whether her true self — whatever that was — was represented in her actions, or whether there was a disconnect between what she thought and what she did. I wondered if maybe in her head she knew how to behave, how to interact with me, how to control her anger, and how to be affectionate and forgiving, but she couldn't put her knowledge into practice because of her injury. Or maybe she didn't know any of those things at all. Maybe she was truly communicating what she thought and felt inside. Maybe this *was* the new Krickitt.

As if the tension in our relationship wasn't enough, we were still getting relentless calls from collection agencies and were dealing with the ongoing legal battle to settle with our auto insurance company. Before our accident, I had never had a conversation with a bill collector. I had only ever written one bad check, and that was only because I had put a deposit into the wrong account by mistake. I was very responsible with my finances, and I had always paid my insurance premiums specifically to avoid a financial meltdown in the unlikely event of a serious accident. Now the meltdown had happened, in spite of my good intentions and responsible actions, and we were getting nowhere with the insurance company that I faithfully paid every month.

Some days the problems were overwhelming, sweeping over me in waves. I was drowning in stress and confusion and anger. I couldn't sleep, I'd had to give up my dream job, and I didn't know how to be a husband to my wife any more. On other days life seemed less black and hopeless. The one thing I could hold onto was our faith in God. For all her random behavior, I know Krickitt had faith that God was in control, as did I. In the depths of our nastiest shouting matches, we were still connected by that thread of faith.

Lying in bed late one night with Krickitt asleep beside me, I came face-to-face once again with the fact that only God could heal our marriage. At that point Krickitt and I could hardly be in the same room together without fighting. And I knew the problem didn't all lie at Krickitt's feet. I needed help. God was going to have to break me down in order to build me back up into the husband I needed to be for her, and I finally realized that someone else was going to have to help me do it. Staring at the ceiling, hearing and feeling Krickitt's steady breathing beside me, I rolled these and other thoughts around in my head. *God, what are you doing with my life? What are you doing with my vow?*

I had stood before God and a church full of people and promised to provide for and protect Krisxan Pappas "through times of challenge and need." I vowed to devote myself to her "every need and desire." I declared I would be faithful. I had said those words with such joy and conviction. I had meant them then, and I would honor them now. I just didn't know how.

But I knew somebody would know how, so I finally took Rob's advice and called the state psychiatric hospital to make an appointment. It felt weird to think of going to a counselor by myself after having been to so many sessions with Krickitt. But I really had no choice. I had been sure I could hold myself together, help Krickitt recover, and get us back on track. I had worked at it for more than a year, and I had not succeeded. I had failed my wife, and it was devastating.

I went to my first appointment with counselor Mike Hill, whose wisdom and insight would soon have an incredible impact on me. He was not your typical therapist. He wasn't stuffy or closed off. What you saw was what you got. He was friendly, open, and absolutely fearless.

I told Mike our whole story, ending with my decision that, while I would never divorce Krickitt, it would be difficult to live together happily, and my best shot might be getting her to the point where she could be self-sufficient and live on her own.

He thought for a minute before asking, "Why do you think Krickitt married you in the first place?"

"Because I'm funny, charming, clever, and handsome," I joked. Mike smiled and didn't respond. He waited patiently for my real answer.

"I guess it's because of the way I treated her," I finally replied. "I was interested in her as a person, not just as a woman I might have a relationship with, and I think she liked that. We were soul mates before we fell in love. There's been a strong spiritual side to our relationship from the beginning. Krickitt has an awesome faith in Christ. In fact, the weekend we met we spent one whole evening reading the book of Job together."

"How do you treat her now?"

"Like a father. Like a coach."

"So she feels like she's married to her father?"

It was my turn to smile. "You got me, Mike. I don't know how she feels. I know she's willing to accept that we're married because everybody keeps telling her we are. And I honestly think she wants to love me as her husband. But deep down, I'm not really sure she knows who I am."

After I had a few sessions with Mike and he had some time to understand our situation, he thought it would be a good idea for Krickitt to come with me to one of the sessions. She agreed, and her talk with Mike turned out to be an answer to prayer, the miraculous event we needed to start getting our lives back in sync.

So Krickitt came to my therapy session.

She and Mike talked a while, and then Mike said, "You know, Krickitt, I don't think you have any memory of meeting, dating, and marrying Kim." Incredible as it seems now, no one had ever said those simple words to her.

Krickitt's face lit up after Mike's revelation. "That's it!" she said excitedly. "That's it! No wonder this has been so weird."

We all understood Krickitt had lost her memory. Her family, friends, and I all knew she didn't remember meeting, dating, or marrying me. What we hadn't realized was that, in spite of countless conversations throughout her rehab, Krickitt didn't truly understand what had happened to her. People had told her over and over that she was married to me, that she really was the woman in our wedding videos, and that she had picked out the china in the cupboard. But nobody had ever explained it as concisely and neatly as Mike did that day in his office.

Krickitt knew her memory had been erased, but she had been in great turmoil because she thought she should know me, but she didn't. What she finally realized was that it was all right not to know me or recognize our china. It didn't mean she was crazy. She wasn't in a dream. She simply couldn't remember our life together because she had amnesia. With that in mind, she wasn't *supposed* to know me. It was impossible. It was not her fault that she couldn't remember any of it.

Does this seem extremely confusing? Imagine what it must have been like for Krickitt.

So Mike came up with a plan. We had already determined that our roles were mixed up. We were living as coach/athlete or parent/child, not as husband and wife. In essence, I had all the control and I expected her to follow my orders. There was little of the give-and-take that should characterize a healthy marriage. So Mike helped us see that we needed to re-establish the equality in our marriage that had been swept away by the events of the previous year and a half. We also had to rebuild a shared history.

"You and Krickitt need a fresh start," Mike explained. "Krickitt doesn't have any stockpile of shared memories with you. Shared memories leave a trail of emotional attachment that she could trace back to the time you met, reliving all the events, emotions, and growth that lead up to a happy marriage. It's an emotional journey she doesn't remember taking, so it's no wonder she looks around and thinks, *How in the world did I get here?*

"A new set of memories that she can remember will build new emotional ties between you. I think the old Krickitt is gone. It's time you got to know the new Krickitt. And it's time for her to get to know you."

"So what do we do now?" I asked.

"How did you get to know the old Krickitt?" he came back.

"We went out on dates. We went to ball games, the movies, had dinner with friends . . ."

"Then get to know the new Krickitt the same way."

"Start dating my own wife?" I wondered aloud.

"It's a way to replace the memories Krickitt has lost," he said. "To her, you don't have a past together, nothing to build a marriage relationship on. It's a second chance to get to know her."

I was excited about the prospect of a second chance with Krickitt. For me, it was a second chance in two ways. First, I got another chance to make things work after the accident. I hadn't done too well with my first opportunity. And second, I had another chance to simply get to know this amazing woman. I had enjoyed doing it the first time, and I was hoping to enjoy it just as much the second time.

So I took Mike's advice and started dating my wife. Las Vegas, New Mexico, isn't nearly as exciting as the more famous town with the same name, but I promised Krickitt that every week we would have date night. The point wasn't to do something exciting, it was to do something together. We ate pizza. We went bowling. We went to ball games. We went to Walmart, where we would let an employee pick out a bag of candy and we would share it with them in the store; when we left, Krickitt would pay for the empty bag. Krickitt appreciated the break in routine, and I liked it too. And we actually got along pretty well on our little excursions. It seemed to be working out pretty well.

However, we did have our moments, and those moments often happened as we were playing golf. The first time we played, we didn't make it through the second hole before Krickitt stomped off in one direction and I drove off in the golf cart in another. We were back in the world of sports, and guess what happened? The coach and father in me had come back out. Needless to say, Krickitt wasn't happy.

When we came back together, Krickitt let me have it. She was tired of me not accepting who she was now. "I'm sorry," I said. "But if you'd quit being such a whiner, you'd do a lot better, and all these people wouldn't be staring at us." That wasn't the response she was looking for. With a withering glance, she stalked off to the parking lot.

As tough as that first golf outing was, we both decided to give it another try. It was a good testing ground for our new relationship. We were forced to figure out how to get along if we wanted to play. The second experience was pretty much a repeat of our first game. Still we tried it again, forging ahead bravely for two or three holes before one or both of us would lose our tempers. After a few tries we could make it all the way through the fourth hole before the shouting began.

Every couple has highs and lows in the dating game and we were no different. Everyone has issues to work through; it just happened that we had to go through it all twice, and the second time was much harder. The general trend during that time, though, was definitely positive. Our dates gave us something to talk about other the accident and its consequences. Since we had more in common now, we relaxed more. We laughed more. We kissed more. The momentum had definitely, miraculously, shifted from a downward spiral to an upward climb.

Krickitt, Mike, and I met regularly to talk about our progress. Mike's plan seemed to be working. Krickitt and I were building a shared past as a foundation for a new future, and our day-to-day relationship was clearly improving, though we still fought way too much. I finally hoped the worst was behind us and could imagine us staying together after all, something that had seemed impossible only a few months before.

Mike's plan didn't end with us dating each other again. He wanted us to have a rededication ceremony. My immediate reaction to the idea of a "second wedding" was that it was out of the question.

I didn't like Mike's suggestion for several reasons. First of all, we were already married. Would a rededication service send a message to others that we thought our first round of dedication had worn out or dried up? I actually saw it as the opposite. It was because of that first dedication — those first vows — that we were still together today. Second, I didn't see any point in going to so much trouble for a purely symbolic gesture. Third, it was yet another big expense at a time when our finances were in shambles.

Krickitt, however, latched onto the idea as soon as Mike suggested it. She explained her point of view to Mike and me. "I've gotten to know my lifetime buddy again," she said, echoing my words when I proposed to her in California, which seemed like a million years ago. "We've had so much fun. How can you not care deeply for somebody who has stood by you like Kimmer has stood by me? I want to remember giving my hand to him in marriage. Another ceremony will give me the memories every wife should have."

While I still wasn't the biggest proponent of this plan, seeing Krickitt so excited and animated made me think maybe I should do it because it would make her happy. Even if it didn't mean as much to me as it obviously did to her, it was something I could do to show her how much I loved her.

"I have snapshot memories of my life just before the accident, but I don't have heart memories," she said as we continued to talk with Mike. "That's what I want to get back, something in my heart.

"I want to remember wearing a big, white

161

wedding dress and having my dad give me away. I want to know what it feels like." That sounded pretty logical to me. After all, if I had lost a memory of meeting a sports hero, I would rather meet him again than just be told about it and be shown the photos.

"When I lost my memory, I lost my feelings for Kim. I had to re-discover what it was about Kim I had fallen in love with before. I can't remember what it was like the first time, but I'm guessing that this time my love has grown in a different way — not that 'fluffy' romantic love, but more of a conscious choice. The fact was, I was married to this man. The feelings came later, and by God's grace I've grown to love him again."

That's when I realized I wasn't the only one who had kept a vow. Krickitt kept her vow to honor and support a man she didn't remember marrying. For better or worse, as she said with a smile: "I'm stuck with you for life. We will make it work. There is no other option."

"You coached me through rehab," she said to me with conviction. "You taught me how to walk again and how to hold a fork. You even helped me go to the bathroom. Now I want you to see me as your wife, not your daughter."

I couldn't have agreed more.

Krickitt wanted to wait until after our insurance problems were settled before going through with our second wedding. I agreed, since it wouldn't be good to have that hanging over our heads on the big day. It was only a few weeks later that we mediated and came to a settlement. Bills were paid up and liens were lifted — one more reason to celebrate a new beginning.

I figured that a new wedding meant a new proposal. I decided I would surprise Krickitt at the fitness center where she worked part-time. On Valentine's Day 1996, I walked into the center with a bouquet of roses, got down on one knee in front of the woman I loved, and as a small crowd gathered, I slipped her wedding ring off her finger and repeated the words I had said nearly three years earlier, "Krisxan, will you be my lifetime buddy?"

Once again, Krickitt Carpenter agreed to marry me, and I slipped her ring back on her finger. I could tell, though, that she was a little disappointed with my lack of creativity. Looking back on it, I can see she was right. The sights, sounds, and smells of an exercise studio aren't exactly the stuff of which romance is made. Even though sports had been such a big part of our lives, I know I blew it.

I had originally agreed to the rededication ceremony in order to make Krickitt happy; but the idea grew on me, and before long I was as excited about another wedding as she was. However, this was not going to be the huge production the first ceremony had been. Instead we wanted something quieter and more intimate.

We found a rustic log chapel at Pendaries, a resort in the little town of Sapello, not far from Las Vegas, that was perfect. It only held about thirty people, but since we were only inviting a few close friends, we figured that would be plenty of room.

As the day approached, Krickitt was the picture of confidence and composure, though she warned us that would likely change on the actual day. "I'm going to be a bawling mess when I walk down that aisle," she predicted. "That's when it's going to hit me — everything that's happened in the last few years."

As always, Krickitt was consistently writing in her journal. The day before our second wedding, she wrote, "Lord, . . . Please open my mind and heart to say the words in my vows you wish. I pray that Kim and I may spend some quality times to-gether sharing, laughing, and caring. I pray for our second honeymoon, that it may really go well. I can't wait. I need your strength, Lord, and your Spirit. Please help me and Kimmer grow closer together. I love you."

Krickitt chose Megan Almquist to reprise her role as maid of honor. Megan was look-ing forward to watching Krickitt make a memory she would hang onto. I chose a dif-ferent best man for our second big day: Krickitt's favorite physical therapist, Scott Madsen. He was the perfect choice because he had played an important role in Krickitt's recovery and his encouragement had helped me through my darkest days.

Some very special people came to share our new beginning with us, many of whom we met as a result of the accident. We were blessed with the presence of DJ Coombs, the EMT who'd overcome her claustropho-bia to treat Krickitt when she was still hang-ing upside down in the car; Bob Grothe, the flight nurse on the helicopter from Gal-lup to Albuquerque when almost everyone had all but given up on Krickitt; and Wayne and Kelli Marshall, the couple who had stopped at the scene of the accident and prayed for us.

So on May 25, 1996, I stood in the front of the little mountain chapel at Pendaries, faced the great love of my life for the second time in the presence of God and a body of witnesses, and spoke with an assurance and love and deepest thanksgiving that I will never be able to describe. I could barely see Krickitt through the tears in my eyes as I pledged myself to her once again.

"Krick, I stand before you once again, re-affirming the commitment of vows I once made. I thank God every day for sparing our lives and providing strength and will to endure these trials and tribulations. Almost three years ago I made a vow before God. And as I stated then and state now with greater love and desire:

"I promise to defend our love and hold it in highest regard. I promise to be forgiving, understanding, and patient. I promise to tend to your every need. I promise to respect and honor you fully.

"Most of all, I promise that no matter the adversaries we may face, I will never ever lose the vow of commitment to protect you, guide you, and care for you until death do us part.

"Only one thing can surpass forever the painful events that we have felt. That is the love I have for you, and I thank the Lord for his guidance and faith in me to love you. I am truly honored to be your husband."

Krickitt's vows were a lot shorter, but no less meaningful.

"Kimmer, I love you. I cherish you as my husband. Thank you for being true to your first vows. I promise to be here for you, to encourage you and comfort you in your time of need. I pray that I may be the wife that the Lord desires for you to have.

"I need you, Kimmer. And I love you."

Krickitt was wearing the same gown she had worn to our first wedding. I, on the other hand, was not able to fit into the same tuxedo. Although we had agreed to use the same rings, as a surprise I had also bought a new ring and planned to put them both on her finger together when the time came.

After I slipped both rings on Krickitt's finger, Megan handed Krickitt my old ring. When she opened her hand, I saw she had also gotten me a second ring. The new one was gold with the Christian fish symbol as a representation of everything the Lord had done in our lives. As she slipped the two rings on where the old one had been, Krickitt gave me the huge smile I had seen so many times before the accident. I was thrilled to see it once again.

I took Krickitt back to the same hotel on Maui that we had gone to on our first honeymoon. As we drove to the beach we saw a sign that read, "Jesus Is Coming Soon." Krickitt told me she'd had a flash memory of it but no context to put it in until now.

We went to the place that had been our favorite spot on the beach during our first trip. "Something clicks," she said, looking at a patio with some tables and chairs scattered across it. She even showed me the table where we had sat nearly three years earlier. "But it's déjà vu minus me," she explained.

We never again tried to jog Krickitt's memory. From that moment on we gave it up to God. Our lives were in his hands, and he was having us look to the future, not to the past. And our future, it turned out, was going to take us places and give us opportunities we never could have imagined.

8
GLOBAL IMPACT

Our two weddings had a lot of things in common: the dress, the rings, the maid of honor, the honeymoon trip. But there was one huge element that was only present at our second wedding: the media. Yes, outlets such as CBS Television, *People* magazine, the *London Times*, ABC News, and *Inside Edition* were there with the hopes of getting a glimpse of our big day.

After the second proposal, we had discovered that people who heard our love story were very encouraged by it. This, in turn, encouraged Krickitt to pray. She asked God to use our story in ways that would show others his amazing love and power. After all, he was the one responsible for us keeping our vows. We weren't still together because of any special traits either of us had; it was all because of God. We couldn't have done it without our faith in him.

Mere days after Krickitt prayed that

prayer, we got a call out of the blue from Van Tate, host of a TV show called *On the Road* on the CBS affiliate in Albuquerque. Van was doing a story on "Whatever Happened to Coach Carpenter?" At the time when I was head coach, I had been the youngest in the NCAA, and a lot of people had interest in my story. When speaking to us on the phone, Van remembered the accident, and he was excited about our plans to have a second wedding ceremony. He wanted to highlight our story on his show.

A few days after Van's show, a reporter from the *Albuquerque Journal* called and wanted to do a story too. On Sunday, March 17, 1996, we were front-page news in Albuquerque under the headline "Love Lost and Refound." The article went into more detail about our accident and Krickitt's rehab, but the main focus was that after all that had happened we were not only still married but were going to renew our wedding vows.

Krickitt and I were both excited to see that the author and editors hadn't glossed over or even completely failed to mention the importance of faith in our lives. On the second page of the story there was a large photo of the two of us praying in front of an open Bible.

The article also included this quote: "I'm not marrying the same person I married three years ago, but I'm not the same person either. For instance, baseball doesn't mean what it used to mean to me. That was part of our old life. We're closer now; we've got a different bond, a more meaningful connection than before. My friends say I've become a religious freak. No, I tell them, I've just seen the miracles that God's work can provide."

We were glad that people were hearing our story and seeing the part God played in it, but we didn't really think of our story as something that was special or compelling enough that it would be of interest to anyone outside of our little corner of New Mexico. We were wrong. We soon got a call from Tom Colbert, the president of a company called Industry Research and Development that looks for human-interest stories in the news and helps local reporters connect with national media. He had seen the article in the *Albuquerque Journal* and asked us if we wanted him to release our story through the Associated Press. He explained that once it was fed to the AP network, it would be available to hundreds of newspapers and other news outlets across the country.

"You need to think carefully about this," he advised us. "Because if we do this, your lives are never going to be the same."

Tom's words sounded almost like a warning. But hadn't it been only a week ago that we were saying, "Lord, we have this great story. How can we use it to show others how amazing you are?" So we talked, thought, and prayed about it, and we felt like it was what God wanted us to do, so we agreed. We honestly didn't think much would come of it, since by that time it had been nearly two and a half years since the accident. We couldn't imagine that our story was big enough for national news. But it turned out that Tom knew what he was talking about. As soon as our story broke nationally, our lives truly did change. But if anyone was equipped to deal with change, we were.

The calls increased in number every day, until the phone would ring again as soon as we hung it up. The day before our wedding there was a feature article about us in the *Los Angeles Times.* And that night Jay Leno even mentioned us in his opening monologue on *The Tonight Show.*

We talked to as many media people as we could during our second "engagement," but it was overwhelming. We had to make some decisions because not only did we need to know how to respond to the various requests we were getting about media coverage for the wedding, but we were also trying to *plan* that wedding. It's no secret that weddings take time to coordinate, but we found that all of our time was being eaten up with dealing with the media.

In the end, we decided to give *Inside Edition* the exclusive video rights to cover the actual wedding ceremony. They had offered to pay for the wedding and honeymoon in exchange for those rights. Though we had finally settled matters with our insurance company, our finances were still very tight, so we felt like *Inside Edition*'s offer was the wisest option for us to take.

Though *Inside Edition* had the exclusive rights to the ceremony, that wasn't all they would cover. They wanted to feature us several weeks before the wedding to give their viewers something to whet their appetites. They sent a reporter and crew to our house in Las Vegas and set up shop in our living room. They captured us on film as we watched the video of our first wedding and as Krickitt looked at pictures and other keepsakes from a day she no longer remembered.

There wasn't a bride's room in the tiny

log church at Pendaries, so Krickitt's parents had parked their RV outside for her to use as a dressing room. True to their name, the *Inside Edition* crew was in there with her, squeezed in with bridesmaids and everybody else, talking to Krickitt about her dress, her feelings about what was happening, and all the other things that go along with a bride's big day.

While *Inside Edition* was the only video publication allowed on the inside of our wedding festivities, there were plenty of other people on the outside. Among many others hoping for a glimpse of us on the church grounds was a photographer from the *London Times* and another from *People* magazine.

We had tried to keep the location of our honeymoon a secret, but we heard a rumor that *Hard Copy* had learned we were going to Hawaii and were going to have a crew waiting for us at the airport in Honolulu. While we wanted to share our story with others, that was not welcome news. We had no desire to share our honeymoon with anyone else, especially a television news show. So I called the airport in Honolulu and explained the situation. We didn't see a trace of them when we arrived.

The staff at the hotel where we stayed on

Maui was under strict orders to keep our presence a secret. We registered under aliases, so they were telling the truth when they told callers that there was no Mr. and Mrs. Kim J. Carpenter registered there. But there was a radio station from California that had guessed we would spend our second honeymoon on the same island as our first one, so they started calling every hotel on Maui trying to find us. They had called all but two when they got to us . . . at 4 a.m. Hawaii time. It obviously wasn't ideal, but we spoke to them. I never heard that interview, but I can guarantee it wasn't one of our best.

Inside Edition's second feature on us ran while we were in Hawaii. As a result, people started recognizing us on the street in Maui. "Hey, didn't I see you guys on TV yesterday?" So much for anonymity. We were thousands of miles from home and people knew who we were. It was a bit surreal.

When we arrived at Los Angeles International Airport for a layover on our way home from Hawaii, we were shocked to see our faces in *Star* magazine. We hadn't realized they were at the wedding, but it didn't take us long to realize which of the people present that day had reported the story and taken the pictures for them. There had been one particularly obnoxious stranger hovering around the front of the church during the ceremony, getting in front of our family video camera and that belonging to *Inside Edition.* We had tried to keep an eye on him and told one of the ushers to make sure he didn't get inside, but in the end there was too much going on to really worry about him. Thanks to our lack of attention, we were now stars of the supermarket tabloids.

We had no sooner returned to Las Vegas than we were flooded with requests and invitations from syndicated TV shows. We wanted to accept as many of the offers as we could, which meant life was going to get more hectic than ever. For the first shows we did, crews came to interview us in New Mexico. It wasn't long before we got invitations to New York and L.A. to be interviewed in person by the hosts. Except for Krickitt's mission trip to Hungary, neither of us had traveled much, so it was a new experience for us. We sometimes traveled to two or three different places in the same week. When we were in Seattle for a show, some Japanese tourists approached us outside the studio. Apparently our story had gone global; they had seen our story on television in their home country. We also learned that we had been featured on a television show in Germany.

We were fortunate to do some television interviews with celebrities we had watched over the years, and we enjoyed meeting them and getting to know them on a more personal level. It was interesting to see what they were like when they weren't on camera.

One of our most memorable interviews was with Sally Jesse Raphael. Her producers asked us to appear on her show because Sally has a son with a head injury caused by a motorcycle crash. Sally saw our story as a way to help educate the public on the devastating effects of such injuries. As tragic as it was, her experience gave us a shared understanding of what a life-changing event a head injury can be. She could talk to us on a deeper level than others could because she knew firsthand what we were going through, and vice versa. Because of this connection she was able to interview us with extra insight and sensitivity.

We also got a call to be on *Oprah.* We were able to share our faith with her audience, which made it possible for us to reach more people at once than we ever had before. We also appeared on Leeza Gibbons's talk show, *Leeza,* and we found that she was truly an elegant and classy lady. In addition, Anne Curry interviewed us on *Dateline* and

Maury Povich and Montel Williams invited us on their shows.

Though we spent much time on the talk show circuit throughout the rest of 1996, we also continued to do interviews with newspapers and magazines. There were major stories published about us in *McCall's* ("The Wife Who Forgot She Was Married") and *Reader's Digest* ("For Better, For Worse"), among others.

During all of our trips we were taken to the best restaurants, chauffeured around town in our own limousine, and generally treated like celebrities for a day or two. The best thing about it, though, was that having a taste of show business was a great way to reaffirm what was truly important to us in life. For all the attention we started getting, we were the same people after we went on TV as we were before. We were just two people trying to work out our lives together, keep our promises to each other, and make sure God was in the middle of it all.

We also got wonderful support from the Christian media. James Dobson of Focus on the Family wrote about us in his "Family News" newsletter in June of 1997. He said:

In this day when the culture teaches us to bail out at the first sign of frustration or pain, it is uplifting to see this young couple work to recapture what they had lost and to remain committed to each other even in the face of tragedy. Their example will, I hope, be relevant to many of my readers who have lost the passion in their marriages — not as a result of brain injury, but from whatever has driven them apart. Perhaps Kim's decision to win Krickitt's affection anew will be especially helpful to those who have misplaced the "memory" of love. If you have been considering a divorce, wouldn't it be better to begin courting your spouse again and seeking to rebuild the marriage from the ground up? That is never easy and I'm sure Kim and Krickitt have not yet faced their final challenges. But it is the right thing to do, and ultimately, the most rewarding response for disengaging husbands and wives. And it is definitely in the best interests of children.

Let me conclude by offering a word of advice to young men and women who will be joining hands in holy matrimony during this summer. . . . I urge each of you to enter into marriage with an unshakable commitment to make it last a lifetime. Let nothing short of death separate what is about to be consummated. When the hard times come (and they WILL come), I hope you will remember the story of Kim and Krickitt who are weathering the storm together — hand in hand and soul to soul. That is God's plan for the family — and for your family.

A year and a half after our second wedding we were surprised to be the cover story for *Christian Reader* magazine's November/December 1997 issue. Soon after that we began working on our first book *The Vow: The Kim and Krickitt Carpenter Story,* which was published by Broadman & Holman Publishers in 2000.

In the midst of the media frenzy surrounding our second wedding, Hollywood came calling. Tom Colbert, who had helped us with media relations from the beginning, stepped in to guide us through the motion-picture industry maze. Several studios wanted to take an option on our story.

After a lot of prayer, we made a decision to go with Paul Taublieb and his LXD Productions. Of everyone we talked to, Paul had the best understanding of what we had been through and what we wanted a movie about us to accomplish. He ultimately got us connected with Roger Birnbaum and Caravan Pictures, which is now Spyglass Entertainment.

After we signed the movie deal in 1996, we prayed for many years about when and if a movie would ever actually be released. Fourteen years later we learned that the movie would, indeed, be produced. *The Vow,* starring Rachel McAdams and Channing Tatum, will be released in the United States and various other countries in February of 2012. Sony Screen Gems will be marketing and distributing the film.

We were invited to visit the movie set during filming and had the opportunity to spend some time with both Rachel and Channing. We thoroughly enjoyed the experience. Four months after shooting wrapped up, we traveled to California to watch the movie that was inspired by the events of our lives. Though many changes were made, as is typically the case when true events are adapted for the silver screen, the basic framework was still in place and Krickitt and I felt it to be an excellent portrayal of the message of our story. I even cried while watching the movie.

We know we have many interviews in our immediate future, surrounding the release of the movie. We look forward to seeing how our story continues to inspire and bless so many. God is the real star of our story, but it has been awesome see how he has used us to make an impact on so many lives.

When our story had first gained national attention from the *Los Angeles Times* and *Inside Edition* in the spring of 1996, a lot of people in the media business told us to take advantage of every opportunity to tell our story because soon we'd be old news and nobody would want to book us.

They couldn't have been more wrong. Here it is, sixteen years later, and millions of people around the world will see a movie inspired by the chain of events that changed our lives forever.

In addition, we have never solicited appearances or interviews, but even before the announcement that the movie would be released, representatives from the media were still contacting us from time to time. People can't seem to get enough of this story, and we've been happy to go anywhere, anytime to tell it. The publicity over the years has also brought a demand for Krickitt and me to speak to churches, marriage enrichment groups, and all sorts of other audiences. Neither one of us had much prior experience with public speaking when we started, but we were willing to do it for the opportunity of sharing what the Lord had done for us. He has answered our prayers and kept our story alive.

9
A FAMILY OF HOPE

In the summer of 1998, Krickitt and I moved to my hometown of Farmington, New Mexico, near the Four Corners. TV reporters arrived at our house before we even got the boxes unpacked. By the end of the week there was a photo of us in the local news section of the *Farmington Daily Times* with a headline reading "Carpenters Keeping 'The Vow': Famous Couple Moves to Town as World Watches," and a sidebar that said "*Dateline* to feature couple on Monday."

In Farmington I became chief administrator of a partnership program between New Mexico Highlands University and the local community college that allowed Farmington residents to take Highlands extension courses. Though it was quite different from my job as a baseball coach, I enjoyed continuing to work for Highlands University.

Krickitt began a part-time job as a lead fitness aide at San Juan College's Fitness Center, which was open to the community. After a few months she decided to make a change and take on a bigger challenge. She began substitute teaching at Kirtland Central High School, and it ended up being nearly a full-time job for her.

After school let out for the summer, Krickitt signed up to volunteer at San Juan Regional Medical Center in their Cardio Pulmonary Rehab department. She really enjoyed the challenge of working with the patients there. After about a month of volunteering, the hospital hired her on to assist in the growing rehab program.

In 1999 we were back on the *Leeza* show where we made a huge announcement: We were having a baby! Leeza was overjoyed for us, and the media machine kicked into high gear once again. At that time we both had jobs, and we were doing interviews and public speaking events whenever we could. That would have been a hectic schedule for anyone, but combined with Krickitt's pregnancy and the stress of knowing that the media would be there for the birth of our baby, we were both really worn down by the time the due date arrived.

On May 3, 2000, Danny James Carpenter

was born at the San Juan Regional Medical Center. He was greeted by family, friends, and hordes of media representatives. Prior to Danny's birth, I had met with key employees at the hospital to work out a plan for security at the hospital. The hospital staff more than came through for us during and after the birth. They were wonderful to work with, and I was truly impressed by their level of concern for our comfort and privacy during our stay.

Within the first five weeks of his life, Danny had made appearances on the *Today Show, Dateline NBC, FOX News, MSNBC,* and other shows. His birth was also announced by *People* magazine. In addition, he was spoiled by the likes of Leeza Gibbons and Ann Curry, who had become true friends over the years and who sent gifts and flowers upon notice of his birth.

Krickitt and I had mixed feelings about all of the interviews and appearances so soon after our son's birth. We were concerned for his well-being, but we also felt like God had given us yet another opportunity to not only share our story, but also to provide some inspiration and hope to people going through their own personal challenges.

Little Danny welcomed his little sister,

LeeAnn Marie, into the world in June of 2003. LeeAnn was named after our friends Leeza Gibbons and Anne Curry, as well as Krickitt's mom, Mary. Danny and LeeAnn are our steadfast reminders that we made the right choice when we stuck together through our tragedy. Had we not done so, our children would never have been born.

Nearly two months after LeeAnn's birth, our lives were thrown into turmoil due to a head injury once again. As most parents know, even a second-long lack of attention to a small child can lead to an accident, and we learned that firsthand. During one of those short lapses of supervision, our baby girl fell and hit her head.

I couldn't believe that for a second time a girl I loved more than life itself had bleeding on the brain and needed to be airlifted to a critical care unit at a hospital in Albuquerque. Unlike my experience with Krickitt, I was allowed to ride in the air ambulance with LeeAnn. After I said good-bye to Krickitt and boarded the aircraft, I spent a nightmarish time watching my critically injured baby daughter and thinking that this accident hadn't been caused by another person. There was nobody to blame for my daughter's injury but her parents.

We neglected a minute detail in her stroller restraint and now she was on the brink of permanent brain damage or even death. Fear, guilt, and anguish pushed heavily on me as we flew over the New Mexico landscape toward Albuquerque.

An agonizing half hour later we landed and ground transport rushed LeeAnn and me to the pediatric intensive care unit at Presbyterian Hospital. I had a horrible sense of déjà vu as I watched my daughter go through many of the same tests and scans her mother had experienced nearly ten years earlier. At least this time I had a better idea of what was going on and what all the monitors and tests were for.

I spent much of the first five hours after LeeAnn's accident alone among strangers. Just as I had been left behind while Krickitt made her life-saving flight, Krickitt had been left to make a middle-of-the-night drive to Albuquerque. She wasn't injured like I had been the first time, but I know she felt the same fear I had on that night all those years ago. When Krickitt arrived at the hospital at 3:00 a.m. after a three-hour drive, I immediately told her how sorry I was.

Later that morning we received the news that the bleeding on LeeAnn's brain had stopped and things were looking fairly good for her. She was sleeping a lot, the way Krickitt had at first, but at no time was she in a coma. The first time she opened her eyes I was relieved to look into them and see life instead of the hollow and emotionless stare Krickitt had given me when she first opened hers.

It wasn't long before we were able to take our baby girl home, and she was quickly back into her usual groove. It took me much longer to recover from my feelings of guilt and from the nightmare I relived during those first few hours. Fortunately, LeeAnn has had no lasting side effects from the accident.

It may come as no surprise that Danny is a baseball superstar, even at the age of eleven. He started playing when he was three years old, and I couldn't help but jump back into coaching, though at quite a different level than before. Danny's team, the "Farmington Fuel," has made it to the American Amateur Baseball Congress World Series four years in a row. I'm very proud of my son and his team for making it that far based completely on performance, not on how much money you can pay to play, as is the case in many baseball organizations.

Danny also wrestles and plays football, basketball, and golf. He has a lot of athletic potential, and Krickitt and I look forward to seeing just how far he wants to take his abilities. He is definitely following in our footsteps, and I hope he will be more like his mom because she has a better work ethic than I do.

LeeAnn is very much like her mother. She will wrap you up in a conversation that goes on and on and on. She is very vibrant and caring, and she loves everyone. It's very touching how our little girl shows concern for her classmates and prays for them to get better when they're sick.

She also enjoys crafts, writing, and reading. In fact, during her first grade year, she read more than three hundred books. Like the rest of us, LeeAnn also enjoys sports and we're excited to see which ones she will choose to stick with. She currently plays softball and basketball, and she enjoys dance. Recently she has even decided she wants to wrestle like her brother. She has also started voice lessons and loves Taylor Swift.

Though many years have passed since our accident, Krickitt continues to improve mentally. It's fun to see her discover new things and become aware of things she hadn't before. However, no one meeting her today has any idea she ever had a severe head injury, unless they know our history.

After Danny's birth, Krickitt stopped substitute teaching and stayed home to take care of our small family. Once the kids had both started school, she jumped right back in to substituting at Farmington High School and has been at it ever since.

As for me, after spending eighteen years in higher education, I moved to the public sector. I have worked for San Juan County since 2005, and in August of 2011, I was named the county's Chief Executive Officer. I work with many great Christian leaders and I enjoy the teamwork and accountability that characterize my work. I also serve as the incoming chairman of the Connie Mack World Series — an amateur baseball tournament.

I decided a long time ago that I wanted to live my life to the fullest. I wanted to try and do everything at least once and then go back and do more of the things I enjoyed the most. After many exciting activities, including SCUBA certification and getting my pilot's license, I feel I have truly lived.

Our family greatly enjoys spending time together. In addition to playing sports, some of our favorite things to do include flying our radio-controlled aircraft and playing with our various pets — four dogs, one cat, one hamster, a wild chipmunk that has made his home in our backyard, and a one-eyed water frog.

We still live in Farmington, where both sets of our parents now reside. My twin brother and his family live here as well. It has been great to have our kids grow up around so much of their family. My only wish is that my older brother would move back so that the Carpenter family would all once again be united. Throughout our ordeal with Krickitt, we learned the importance of close family ties, and we're glad our children know and love their extended family.

Although Krickitt has never gained any memory of meeting, dating, or marrying me (the first time), our life today could not be better. After all we have been through enduring the trials and tribulations that have confronted us, we know there will be more to come. That's just how life works. But we have a great sense of appreciation and thankfulness for what God has given us. We have been truly blessed.

Eighteen years have now passed since our accident, but we are reminded of it every day. Unlike the first few years of our trials, our memories no longer bring about uncertainty, fear, or anger, but instead a great sense of purpose. God has given us such an amazing opportunity to reach out to others. We continue to speak to others about our experience, and we occasionally get phone calls from someone who has read or heard about our story. From time to time we also get calls from people whose loved ones have been in traumatic events and who need our support and encouragement. Though those moments are hard for us only because I know the horror of what they're going through, we know that walking with others who are where we once were is a way we can give back and give purpose to the events of our lives.

A good friend of mine, songwriter Billy Simon, penned the lyrics of a song titled, "A Man You Would Write About" that was recorded by the Christian singing group 4Him. In that song, he talks about how he wants to be a man that could be written about and still be read about one thousand years later. To me, that would be the ultimate reward — to have lived a life so full of faith that people will still read about you in a thousand years. However, I don't see the recognition as the reward; instead the reward is that you've been provided a means to bless and inspire others to help them live the fullest life they can.

A publicist once told me we've been seen or heard by an estimated six hundred million people around the world. That's twice the population of the United States. But even though we have been given an amazing opportunity to inspire many, the two people I most want to inspire are my children. I cannot wait for the day when they are able to read this book and understand all that their mother and I have been through. I believe that sharing life's experiences and learning from them creates a strong family foundation. What strengthens it even more is having God at the center of it all.

My father once told me, "Give back what was given to you." That has been my goal, and the greatest blessing has been to watch my children give to others before worrying about their own desires. I have seen my little girl donate all the money in her piggy bank to a Christian radio station that shares God's Word on the airwaves. I have seen my son stand up for the weak and pay dearly for it from a bully. I have seen the two of them give up a favorite toy to a little child who had nothing. The two of them continually amaze me as they put others first by giving, praying, and reaching out to the friendless.

As my children grow, I continually pray that Krickitt and I will raise them in the way God wants us to. We realize that one of the best things we can do for them is to be good examples. Do we always succeed? No. I know I have much to change. Yes, I have failed in making my vow to always respect Krickitt. I still yell at her from time to time and I feel bad about it. But I do know my convictions will continue to remind me of what I need to work on, and with God's help we do our best and rejoice when Danny and LeeAnn make good choices.

Our family lives by three sayings. The first is that we "do the right thing." If you were to walk up to one of my kids on the street and say, "Remember . . ." they will respond with, "do the right thing." Our second saying is, "It's important to give it all you got." We have learned that life is precious, so while we're here we need to give all we have. And our third saying is, "I got gaps, and together we fill them." Think about that for a moment. We all have things that we're good at and not-so-good at, but together we fill each other's gaps. When we work together and complement each other by filling in the gaps, we can achieve our dreams hand in hand. I believe that as our family lives out those three things, we can give to others what has been given to us.

Jesus said, "It is more blessed to give than to receive" (Acts 20:35). I believe that wholeheartedly. But I also believe that in order to truly give, you must know what it is to truly receive. When tragedy strikes you, as it did to us, don't cut yourself off from the world. Instead, reach out to your friends and family, and to God. Then you will know what it is like to receive, and as a result you will know how to give to others.

I wouldn't have thought it was possible, but I love Krickitt more today than I did on our first wedding day. She is an absolutely amazing woman. I can hardly imagine what faith it took for her finally to believe it when everybody kept telling her she was married to me. "God wanted me to be married to this person," she said. "Everybody said I was, and one day, looking in the mirror, I was convicted by the Lord that it was the truth.

"I trusted God when I married Kim, so I knew I'd get to know this guy that I married. I don't look back at what is lost. The media does, but I don't live like that. I fix my eyes above."

Krickitt and I were given a second chance at life together, and neither one of us will ever take each other or our marriage for granted. We had two weddings and the rings to go with them, and we also celebrate two wedding anniversaries every year. Both of those days mark new beginnings for us. We don't dwell on the bad times but look ahead to the amazing things we know God still has in store for us. Krickitt will never have a memory of falling in love or of our courtship and marriage. But she says that what she felt as a bride the second time was a deeper love than most wives experience in a lifetime. Our unique experiences, as awful as they were at the time, have given us a stronger bond than we would have had without them.

I think what has kept our story alive all this time is that it is a story of hope, which is always in short supply and high demand. It would have been so easy for either of us to give up during the long and sometimes dark years during and after the accident, but with God's help we didn't. I often think about the story of Job that Krickitt and I read the first time we met each other. There were many times when I identified completely with this poor servant who went from a life of plenty and happiness to the pit of despair. Yet the Lord brought him through it and eventually heaped riches on him far greater than what he had lost. I don't think I could hold up under the trials that Job had to endure. But I think I have some sense of what he went through, and my life is no less a miracle than his was.

I'm no hero. I have made mistakes just like anyone else has, and I wouldn't be who I am today without my faith and trust in him. This story is not about me, and it's not about Krickitt. It's about the Lord and how he brought my wife and me through a terrible time to a life that is greater than we could have ever imagined. It's about a commitment not only to the Lord but also to each other.

As this book comes to an end, our lives will continue on. As you close the back cover to this book, I want you to remember that in life you will encounter some very tough times, but you can find your strength in God. If there is something missing in your life, seek the Lord. If you once had him in your life and now he seems far away, guess who moved? He is still there; just go to him. He loves you with an everlasting love, and through obedience to him all com-

mitments will endure.
We made a vow.

ACKNOWLEDGMENTS

From Kim

Life sometimes will deliver adversity, and when it comes our strength derives from our faith in God and our family and friends who bestow a sense of stability that can only come from the love and support they give. I want to thank my parents, Danny and "Moose," for teaching me the discipline of living with accountability during the most difficult time of our lives. Kelly and Kirk, I look forward to spending time and growing old side by side the way we grew up. I am grateful for the women behind my brothers, who are a total blessing, not only to them but also to the Carpenter name. And Krickitt, you are my rock that has been there through thick and thin to catch me when I stumble.

To the doctors, nurses, EMTs, and the many others who helped us through our time of turmoil, our gratitude will always uphold you in our memories. To my friends and colleagues, you've been by our side all the way and you have brought much joy in knowing that you are a part of us.

Finally, Danny and LeeAnn, you are the joy of my life. You fill my heart with warmth knowing you not only will carry on our legacy, but you will be a blessing to many you will encounter. Reach for your dreams and help others along the way.

I love you all for making me complete.

— Kim Carpenter

From Krickitt

Life is a gift from the Lord and he is our refuge and strength in good times and bad, in sickness and in health. He has blessed us by creating individuals that have played such an instrumental role in our lives.

To my parents Gus and Mary Pappas, I thank you from the bottom of my heart for the never-ending love, support, and encouragement you have always shown me. In your fifty-plus years of marriage, you have displayed the meaning of a vow. To my brother Jamey, you are a tower of strength and knowledge and an example of Christ, like no other. I love you "Mamey."

To my Southern California girlfriends, Megan, Lisa, Katie, Heather, and "Stussy,"

I thank you for helping me to learn what it really means to be a Christian and how to grow in my relationship with Christ. You are my "sister friends" forever. Dolan, we will always be teammates and our time together at CSUF will always be cherished. To the sport of gymnastics, you and all of my coaches have taught me what it means to work hard, endure, and persevere through the toughest of challenges and pain.

I also want to thank the doctors, nurses, therapists, and counselors who played a vital role in saving my live and aiding in my recovery. To all of my family, in-laws, friends, and the City of Las Vegas, New Mexico, you exemplify the true gift of friendship and giving. For that I will forever be grateful.

My husband Kimmer, I love you with a never-ending love. On September 18, 1993, I made a promise to keep. Thank you for staying true to your vows and loving me with an unconditional love just like Jesus. You are a rock and a truly amazing individual. You are a wonderful husband and father. To my children Danny and LeeAnn, you are my precious blessings from above. I love you and I pray you seek the Lord with all of your hearts. He loves you eternally.

Thank you, Lord Jesus. You are the reason

I did the right thing and gave it my all. May you receive all of the glory and honor.

— Krisxan "Krickitt" Pappas Carpenter

"I can do all things through Christ who strengthens me." (Philippians 4:13)